MASTERS
in the New Energy

Adamus Saint-Germain

Masters in the New Energy

Copyright © 2007 by CCIP, Inc.

CRIMSON CIRCLE

Published by Crimson Circle Press,
a division of the Crimson Circle Energy Company, Inc.
PO Box 7394
Golden, Colorado USA
Contact: customerservice@crimsoncircle.com
Web: www.crimsoncircle.com

All rights reserved. Up to 250 words from this book may be quoted or reprinted without permission, with proper credit given to Masters in the New Energy by Geoffrey Hoppe. Do not reproduce by any mechanical, photographic or electronic process.

Crimson Circle™, Adamus Saint-Germain™, DreamWalker™ and Shaumbra™ are trademarks of CCIP, Inc., Incline Village, Nevada USA. All rights reserved.

ISBN 154416372X

First Printing, September 2007
Second Printing: April 2017

Printed in the United States of America

Cover Design: Geoffrey Hoppe and Adamus Saint-Germain
Book Design and Layout: Geoffrey Hoppe
Transcription: Jean Tinder
Editing: Geoffrey Hoppe and Jean Tinder
Proofing: Jean Tinder

*Dedicated to Shaumbra.
Their journey has inspired
New Energy consciousness
on Earth and elsewhere.*

CONTENTS

Acknowledgments 9
Introduction 11
About Adamus Saint-Germain 13
The Ascension Symbol 15
About Geoffrey Hoppe 17
About the Crimson Circle 19
Glossary 21

Old Masters, New Masters 23
Trust 27
Elegantly Simple 33
Self First 37
All Energy Serves 39
No Compromise 41
Choice 43
Self Containment 45
More on Trust 47
Illusion 49
Acceptance 51
The Unknown 53
Facets and Layers 57
No Expectations 61
No Force 63
Creation 67
Discernment 69
Grandness 73
Ascended Masters 75
More on Acceptance 77
God 81
The Magic of Mastery 87
Trusting, Knowing and Mastery 93
Questions and Answers 99

8

ACKNOWLEDGMENTS

Special blessings to all who participated in the *Masters of the New Energy* sessions in Amsterdam, The Netherlands, March 24 - 25, 2007:

Garret Annofsky	Sinka 't Hooft	Borgred Schotborgh
Joyce Arbouw	Geoffrey Hoppe	Milan Sekulic
Jamina Baek	Denise Hulsmans	Mannie Sommers
Carla Bak	Christine Jacobus	Oddmund Sorgaard
Yvonne Bakker	Esther Jonker	Jan Sprong
Otto Bengsch	Renate Kaya	Gisela Steimel
Linda Benyo	Marianne Keuning	Cindy Stokhorst
Irene Berger	Edwin Kolpa	Jacqueline Thevissen
Mette Bjorgen	Emmie Koster	Jean Tinder
Maria Bogers	Margreet Koster	Tina Tjiang Leroy
Anita Boom	Matthias Kreis	Melanie Trankner
Wessel Boom	Martin Kuhnle	Bodil Valentiner
Wilma Bot	Christa Kuijpers	William van Brussel
Ineke Brandenburg	Paulus Kuiper	Els van den Heuvel
Eva Breitfuss-Langkammerer	Andriana Landegent	Arnoud van der Maas
Marc Breitfuss-Langkammerer	Jim Landegent	Peter van Dijk
Adrienne Brock	Ronaldfrederik Lapre	Simone van Glabbeek
Fiona Brookes	AnneClaire Loogman	Carin van Onna
Jan Brouwer	Tommi Makela	Wim van Onna
Jan Buijse	Paula Silvia Marin	Marieke van Ravensberg
Kristina Buitkamp-Moebius	Elisabeth Mayer	Katharina van Rhijn
Eniet Castillion	Petra Mensink	Roelanda van Vliet
Jose Cox	Kristina Menzel	Josephine Veering
Yvonne Davids	Maryam Mildenberg	Martine Verhek
Yvonne de Bruijn	Charlotte Mogensen	Merel Verkerk
Willemina de jager	Carsten Mortensen	Sabrina Vink
Cora de Jong	Leja Nauta	Ewout Vis
Diana de Reus	Marjolein Neefjes	Kay von Randow
Mieke de Graff	Helene Nielsen	Sarah Vosse
Norma Delaney	Jurgen Obermayer	Paul Voulon
Lisella Deligia	Birthe Signe Julie Olesen	Imelda Vrijenhoek
Paul Demaerel	Maluna Orting	Mayke Vullings
Suzanne Dijkstra	Pieter Ouddeken	Addy J.H. Wartena
Moniek Evertsen	Eve Palmer Nicoll	Yvette Welsch
Lydia Frankenhuis	Iris Pauwels	Rieke Westerveld
Nicole Gadet	Lea Peeraer	Gitta Weytjens
Anja Gijsbers	Jegi Pekkala	Marysia Wilczewska
Veronika Gschwentner	Marijke Princen	Rolf Wild
Markus Gyger	Ellen Pronk	Laurens Willekes
Lea Hamann	Ruben Proost	Thijs Willekes
Gerrit Heijn	Franke Rebecca	Joyce Witteman
Gudrun Heumann	Wolfgang Riedl	Elske Wouters
Sandra Heuschmann	Rudy Robertus	Jacky Wynants
In Sook Hille	Marianne Rombouts	Heike Zeitlmann
Ingrid Homveld	Anneke Scholten	Piet Zwarthoed

Introduction

Early in the spring of 2007, in the city of Amsterdam, Netherlands, Adamus Saint-Germain, an Ascended Master with a long and colorful history, called together a group of New Energy Masters and Teachers. In his opening message, channeled through Geoffrey Hoppe, Saint-Germain revealed that the purpose of this very special gathering was to write a book. The book would be called *"Masters in the New Energy"* and would be a gift of wisdom and inspiration to those humans who choose to step into mastery in this time of great and profound change on the earth. The energy and information given would have its foundation in the wisdom of the ones who had already gone through the process of becoming Masters of the New Energy, helping to lead the way for those who follow. Therefore, during this gathering of Masters, Saint-Germain brought together the collective energy of the group and channeled it into the material which has now become the book you hold in your hands.

This process of collecting the energy of the group and speaking it back through one voice is called a Shoud. Therefore this book is a Shoud of the energies of Adamus Saint-Germain and each of the New Energy Masters who answered the call and gathered together in Amsterdam, Netherlands, the City of the Masters.

The original audio recordings of Saint-Germain's messages were transcribed into text and only lightly edited for ease of reading. No other changes or additions have been made to Saint-Germain's original words.

About ADAMUS SAINT-GERMAIN

Saint-Germain (also sometimes referred to as Master Rakoczi) is a spiritual Master of the Ancient Wisdom credited with mystical powers and longevity. He is also identified with the real life person known as the Count of St. Germain (1710–1784) who lived throughout Europe in the 18th century and was active in many of the Mystery Schools of the time. He adopted his name as a French version of the Latin "Sanctus Germanus," meaning "Holy Brother." Saint-Germain teaches that the highest alchemy is the transformation of one's human consciousness into the divinity of the Higher Self.

Over the years, much has been written and many stories told of this intriguing, somewhat enigmatic figure in history. He is a remarkable being who has manifested in many lifetimes and identities on Earth. In his lifetime as St. Germain, he was born in an area now known as Spain to a Jewish Portuguese father and a mother of royal Spanish lineage. He traveled throughout Europe counseling kings and other royalty, and was known as a great alchemist – a great mover of energy.

In 2005 Saint-Germain came to the Crimson Circle organization as a guest of Tobias, another Ascended Master, channeled by Geoffrey Hoppe. After Tobias' reincarnation to the physical realms in July 2009, Saint-Germain took over his teaching and guidance role with the Crimson Circle. In his work with the Crimson Circle, he refers to himself as Adamus Saint-Germain in order to differentiate his contemporary teachings related to embodied ascension from his previous work and previous channelers. Adamus is a unique facet of Saint-Germain's oversoul. His style is provocative, entertaining and deeply insightful. His passion is to assist those who have clearly chosen embodied enlightenment in this lifetime, yet are faced with the myriad distractions and doubts that stem from today's intense mental focus and programming coupled with the density of mass consciousness.

Saint-Germain's ASCENSION SYMBOL

According to Adamus Saint-Germain, the "spade" is the symbol of ascension. He defines ascension as the acceptance and integration of our human nature with our divine origins. When this occurs, karma is released from our life path and we complete our series of lifetimes on Earth. After our last embodiment on Earth, we go to what he calls the "Third Circle" where we become full, conscious Creators. The Creator does not need energy to exist; they do not need to be connected with anyone and anything in order to define themselves. It is the realization of the compassionate "I Am" state of Being.

The spade, according to Adamus, represents the outward expansion of consciousness, beyond the limitations of the human dimensions. The inverted spade, pointing downward, represents the descending of our angelic nature to the denser vibrational energies of Earth. The inverted spade also represents the "heart" or love that we, as angels, have shared by agreeing to embody in physical reality for the good of All That Is.

Historically, the spade is said to represent the cosmic tree, or life, and its antithesis, death. Saint-Germain says that the primary element of the spade is the shape of the heart, which represents the unification of the masculine/feminine, light/dark, human/divine and our other dualistic aspects.

Saint-Germain created the upward-downward spade symbol used throughout this book to express the journey from the angelic realms to embodiment on Earth, and finally our ascension into the Third Circle.

About GEOFFREY & LINDA HOPPE

Geoffrey Hoppe: The early spiritual curiosity of a young man was all but forgotten as he served a few years in the US Army as a Public Information Specialist at the NASA Ames Research Center (Mountain View, California), and then stepped into the business world. After finding his way to senior management positions in several advertising agencies, Geoffrey started his own marketing company in Dallas, Texas at the ripe old age of 28. Later on, he co-founded an aviation telecommunications company (provider of Internet services for business jets and commercial airlines, now known as Gogo), serving as Vice President of Sales and Marketing until 2001. In a stroke of ironic prescience, Geoffrey holds three patents for multidimensional telecommunications technologies, as well as numerous trademarks and copyrights.

Linda Hoppe: A gifted artist and highly creative by nature, Linda graduated Summa Cum Laude and went on to teach Art Education, even writing a ground-breaking curriculum for Texas' first high school honors Art Education program. Her artistic talents landed her a job as Fashion Merchandise Manager with a Fortune 500 company, helping to set the styles and designs for each upcoming season. She also served as manager for Geoffrey's marketing consulting company for several years.

Destiny: Geoffrey & Linda met in high school and got married in 1977 on the day the first Star Wars movie premiered. Twenty years later, an angel named Tobias introduced himself to Geoffrey during an airplane flight. After talking and learning together for an entire year, Geoffrey finally told Linda about his invisible friend. Soon after, Tobias started working with clients of a local psychologist, providing deep insights into past lives and current challenges.

In late summer 1999, a few friends were invited to listen as To- bias spoke through Geoffrey, assisted by Linda. It was the beginning of the Crimson Circle, an organization that they would soon spend every waking moment trying to keep up with. Since then, Crimson Circle has grown into a multinational organization, with Geoffrey & Linda traveling the globe conducting numerous workshops and events each year.

They didn't see it coming, but looking back in hindsight, they wouldn't change a thing in this most extraordinary lifetime.

About THE CRIMSON CIRCLE

I've often been asked, "What is the Crimson Circle?" Words escape me. My tongue gets twisted and my brain starts to spin. How can I describe something so deep – yet simple – and something so outside the realm of normal human thinking? How can I share the thousands of stories about humans around the world coming into their embodied enlightenment, and what the heck is embodied enlightenment anyway?

I used to launch into a long explanation, oftentimes losing my listener when I tried to explain the quest for truth, the wisdom of the Ascended Masters, our *real* purpose for being here on Earth at this time, the dynamics of channeling, the difference between consciousness and energy... well, you get the point. I got way too mental.

Now I just say, "You know what it's like... when you know there's more to life, but you just don't know what it is? That's what the Crimson Circle is about." Somehow people just get it. It saves me a lot of anguish and it saves them a lot of tedious explanation.

And, there is something more to life, no matter what your five senses and mind tell you. There is a Beyond and you're not crazy for thinking that there is. You were just trying to find it with your current senses. Once you allow yourself to go beyond your current senses, you'll come to realize that *there is so much more*.

Learn more about the Crimson Circle at www.crimsoncircle.com

~ Geoffrey Hoppe, channeler for Adamus Saint-Germain

GLOSSARY

Adamus Saint–Germain A master, an angel, a professor and a teacher from the Crimson Council who is delivering inspiring messages for New Energy consciousness.

Cauldre The name Tobias and Adamus Saint-Germain call Geoffrey Hoppe. This is not his "spirit name," rather a nickname used. Pronounced Ka–ool'–dra.

Channeling When a nonphysical entity or angel communicates through a human. The human translates the entity's "thought packets" into words for others to hear or read.

Crimson Circle The group of humans involved in this spiritual journey, preparing to become teachers to others on the journey.

Crimson Council A celestial teaching order, including Tobias, Adamus Saint–Germain, and other angels, assisting us on our journey.

Gnost Gnost is our "creative solution," that part of us that solves problems beyond the capabilities of the mind. It is the 4th "leg" of our human chair: balancing the mind, body, spirit and gnost.

New Energy The new consciousness and vibration of Earth that allows the integration of our divine nature into our human nature. Also, the transition from the physics of "duality" or "2" into the "quad physics" or energy of "4."

Quantum Leap Tobias says that on September 18, 2007 humanity experienced a quantum leap in consciousness; a time where everything began moving at such a fast rate that consciousness no longer follows the old linear path. Instead, the quantum leap in consciousness allows for a new level of creativity, invention, scientific discovery and personal transformation.

Shaumbra The name Tobias uses for the group of humans going through the awakening process. Tobias tells us the term originated during the times of Yeshua ben Joseph (Jesus), when people many of them Essenes would gather for spiritual meetings. Loosely translated in old Hebrew, the first portion of the word Shaumbra is pronounced "shau–home." "Shau–home" means home or family. The second portion of the term is "ba–rah," which means journey and mission. When these terms are put together, it is "shau–home–ba–rah" which means family that is on a journey and experience together. Tobias says that in the biblical times, a "shaumbra" was also a scarf or shawl that was worn by either male or female. It was a distinctive crimson color that let the others know it was time to meet. Pronounced "Shom–bra."

Shoud A Shoud occurs when the energy and consciousness of two or more people are combined to great a group message. Adamus Saint-Germain, Tobias and Kuthumi gather the group energy during their frequent get-togethers with Shaumbra and the group message is then channeled by Geoffrey Hoppe.

OLD MASTERS, NEW MASTERS

I am, yes I am, Adamus Saint-Germain, the Master.

Let's talk for a moment about Masters. The term "Master" is thrown around and used openly and freely and there have been many, many Masters in the past. But the Masters of the past are different than the Masters of the New Energy. So often the Masters of the past had to go through extreme suffering to become a Master. They had to deny their bodies, they had to literally deny their human existence in order to look deeper into their spirit; in order to separate what was human from what was spirit; what was real from what was illusion; what was the battle of the ego from what was the blessing of being human. So many of the Masters that you have heard and read about endured this grand suffering, becoming martyrs as well as Masters. There is no need for that in the New Energy.

The New Energy Master understands that *mastery is about being human*. They understand that it is about integrating all energies into themselves. The New Energy Master understands the principle of Joy, and releases the old concept of suffering. Many of the Masters in the past were isolated. They went off alone, away from the cities, away from their families. They lived as hermits in the woods, on a desolate island or in a forsaken part of the country where no other humans lived, perhaps justifying it by saying that they were getting back in touch with nature. The Masters of old had to leave the presence of other humans in order to truly discover themselves.

However, the New Energy Master understands that it is essential to be a part of humanity, to be a part of the community. The New Energy Master understands that isolation and separation do not serve the needs of the others, the ones who are ready for teachers. So the New Energy Master learns to be the Master while existing in this human reality, surrounded by other humans; while working in everyday jobs;

while traveling; while going to the same stores or perhaps even the same churches as other humans.

There will be times that you need to be alone, there will be times you need to recharge your energy, but the New Energy Master understands it is important to live among other humans. It is important to participate in human existence for how can you teach if you are on some remote island? How can you teach if you are isolating yourself in some distant place? How can you be available to humanity if you are sitting on some mountain top, secluded and difficult to get to?

Many of the Masters in the past studied – hard. They read the ancient texts, they read the philosophies, they studied the religions. They spent most of their years in school and even as they became older they studied and studied and studied, still trying to find their way to enlightenment. They felt that the more they absorbed, they more they studied, the more they knew – this would put them closer to being a Master.

There are very, very few Masters who truly made it this way, though many, many have tried. They all found one thing in common: it brought them so much into the mind that they ignored their true feelings. Sooner or later, the Masters of the past who partook in this rigorous study found that they had to let it all go. A beautiful example of that is Kuthumi Lal Singh. He studied and studied in the universities, trying to study his way to enlightenment, until it literally drove him crazy. He had to release it. He had to understand that all of the book knowledge in the world would never give him the true enlightenment that comes through the feelings and through the gnost, the Divine Intelligence.

Masters of the New Energy have already studied. You've read the books, you've gone to the courses, you've read all the old wisdom teachings. Has it solved the issue? Perhaps is has been pleasurable, perhaps you have enjoyed it now and then, but sometimes you get so absorbed in the study that you forget that you already are the Master. You get so complex, trying so hard to find the intellectual answers, that you forget the answers are already within. You get so engrossed in the search, so focused on the path, that you forget all of the answers are already within you.

So it's not about studying everything that you can find, looking for the answers. By all means study if you enjoy that, if it's pleasurable to you, but, as you have already discovered, you're not going to find the answers that way.

Many of the Masters of the past practiced extreme discipline, disciplining their mind, disciplining their body. They felt that if they focused their energy in a very extreme way (through severe discipline) they could become clear and focused like a laser beam and somehow that would give them enlightenment. But in truth, many of them were just torturing themselves and denying their full existence. It did work, to some extent, for Masters of the past because that was the energy they were in. The energy hundreds or thousands of years ago was much thicker than it is now. It was much more dense, much more difficult to work with and there was a need by aspiring Masters to have this discipline, otherwise they would be caught up in the density of consciousness.

However, in the era that you exist in right now you don't need this extreme discipline. You don't need to deny yourself things that are a part of life. You don't need to be afraid of any of these things around you. There are many who fear that if they partake in certain joys and pleasures of life that it will distract them, that they will get caught up in these things, become addicted to them and forget about their true spiritual path.

Perhaps *you* have blocked yourselves from the true joy of life because you were afraid to partake of its pleasure. Perhaps your soul passion, which is to be a Teacher of the New Energy, had you feeling that these things would distract you, so you literally shut down your own House of Life. But now, in this New Energy, you can open all of these things up.

Perhaps you have been caught up in the past with something like drinking too much alcohol and now you're afraid of it. Perhaps you've been caught up with anger and now you try to lock the door on your own anger and shut it out. Perhaps you've been caught up with drugs or other addictions and you've tried to hide or run from these things because you thought they were grander and stronger than you.

I'm going to ask you, as a Master in the New Energy, to let all of that go – because *none* of these things are grander than you. *You* are the Master. *You* decide. *You* choose. *You* determine how you want it. *You are the Master.*

A Master in the New Energy is quite different than the Master of the past. It doesn't do any good to go back and study the old Masters because they existed in their time and in their era for a specific reason. There were a few true Masters in the past. Yeshua (Jesus), for instance, was a Master two thousand years ago. He was also a changeworker – just like you – and he was the example, the one that stood out from the rest. He represented the Christ Consciousness on earth at the time, the One who represented the Many, because the energy at the time called for that. There could not be many Masters, there could only be a few.

It is different now in this New Energy. It is time to have many Masters all across the world because it is time for each culture, each region and each community to see that there is a Master present. It's time to have many Masters all across the world to help anchor the energy of the new, to anchor the energy of an expanded consciousness, and to anchor this energy of the Christ seed which is blossoming on earth right now.

This is the time for many Masters, not just a few.

Being a Master, surprisingly, does not carry the tremendous responsibility that you might think it does. In this book we'll get into some of the details of what the Master is, how the Master relates to his or her self, to his or her internal environment, and to the world.

TRUST

First and foremost, above all, the single grandest principle of being a Master is trust in self. Trust. It is the essence of this book.

Humans have lost trust with themselves. It is like they are living in a nightmare and have isolated themselves in a tiny, tiny little room. They do not trust their bodies, they only trust a small portion of their mind and they have little or no trust in their spirit and their gnost. Humans place their trust in everything outside of them and even that changes frequently because as soon as humans learn to trust something outside of them they quickly learn to distrust it for they learn that it is not necessarily built on a platform of perfection. They learn that the pedestal can come tumbling down at any time and this causes them to trust even less.

Take your leaders, for instance. A new leader comes along, you are excited, you have hope, you feel that change is imminent. But as this leader comes to represent the overall consciousness of humanity or that land or that particular village, you soon learn that this leader is as prone to mistakes as you. Perhaps this leader doesn't have any more vision than you. Perhaps they are caught up in some type of scandal with drugs or sex or money, these things that have to do with power. Once again your level of trust crashes – until you find somebody new who promises something, somebody else who you can temporarily trust. So, over the course of many, many years, many, many lifetimes, you have fallen out of trust with yourself as well as with things outside of you.

The Master trusts themselves implicitly.

The Master understands and trusts their body for they know that the body is designed to heal and repair itself in miraculous ways. But you have fallen out of trust. You put your trust in some doctor, in some clinic, in some healer, but *they* don't trust themselves either and then it perpetuates. This whole thing of mistrust goes on and on and on.

Perhaps you try to be psychic or intuitive but the answer doesn't always come back the way that you think it should. Perhaps it isn't the "correct" answer – or at least what you think would be correct – and then you don't trust your own inner feelings or your own inner guidance either.

So what do you do? You pray. You pray to some unknown god. You pray to angels. You pray to Tobias. (Very few of you pray to me!) You pray to these Beings who do hear you, who love you, but who cannot do it *for* you. They can only support *your* decisions and *your* choices.

So you fall out of trust with the things in the other realms, with Spirit, and each time you fall out of trust you isolate yourself more and more. You restrict your energy flow. Instead of allowing a lot of life-giving energy to come in and pass through you, you allow only a small amount, only enough to sustain you, to barely get you by. You only let in enough to allow you to survive and exist.

The Master of the New Energy trusts *everything* about themselves. Perhaps that may sound easy but it can be very challenging.

Take a deep breath right now.

How much do you trust *yourself*? Nobody else, yourself?

Do you trust your body to heal itself? To re-balance itself when disease comes in? Do you trust your body to serve you each day without rebelling, without fighting back, without dying off? Probably not. Very, very few humans do.

Do you trust your mind? Do you trust your mind to have access to the answers you need for everyday life, to be able to bring through any information that you need? Do you trust your mind to give you information that you've never even studied about, that you've never known before? Your mind can do that because, through your spirit, your mind has access to the Universal Library where all things exist that have ever been known and ever been created. Your mind isn't just limited to itself and what you have studied, it is a processor for *all* information.

Do you realize right now, if you totally trusted your mind you could have access to very deep and complex mathematical formulas – and you would actually understand them? You could have access to the understanding of the space between the space, to what happens in the inter-dimensional levels. You could have an intellectual understanding of all of these things if you truly trusted your mind. But you have blocked off your mind, you have limited it, rejected it and put walls and barriers and roadblocks along the way. You thought it was your mind driving you crazy. You thought it was your mind that was betraying you so you have closed it off.

Do you trust your spirit? Sitting right here in this moment, do you trust your own spirit? *Would you give your life to your spirit right now?* Probably not. You may give it to Tobias or Kuthumi, probably to Quan Yin. But would you give your life and your existence, your soul – *your eternal life* – to your own spirit right now? Probably not, because you don't even know what your spirit is, much less what your soul is.

You feel that your spirit has never truly been there for you when you have called out to it. When you've cried out at night to your spirit – to you, God – it hasn't been there. It doesn't speak a language, it doesn't have arms and hands, it doesn't perform miracles in the way you would like, so you've learned not to trust even your spirit. Plus you have been trained and educated and controlled into believing that you will not reunite with your spirit until you die so you've shut the door on that part of you. You have shut out your own spirit.

So what do you have left? Little or no trust in your body, in your mind, in your spirit – and actually deep and underlying distrust of God because the God that you were taught about in your early years was angry, was judgmental and *didn't answer your calls for help*. So what do you have left? Very, very little. You live a small, small existence.

There are only a few parts of you that you have learned to trust somewhat. You know you can get yourself up in the morning, for the most part. You know you can get yourself to work, maybe. You know you can feed yourself, but you don't even trust what you're eating. You know you can get by in a very limited way but you are afraid to truly open up to the grand potentials that exist because you don't trust yourself.

The Master comes to trust themselves at *every conceivable level* without outside help, without outside intervention, and that takes a bold, daring and courageous move. Having implicit trust in yourself takes courage beyond anything that you have done in human life before. This trust alone is the greatest part of being a Master for it is this trust in self that will result in all of the other things that we're going to talk about relating to mastery. But you must cross this bridge of trust in self *first*.

Take a deep breath.

You can't force yourself to trust yourself. You can't demand it, you can't work out a program or a plan or a method for it. It just happens when you *choose* it. Perhaps it will be step by step, degree by degree, but you're going to find that this is the grandest, most profound thing you have ever done – this coming back into trust with yourself.

I, Saint-Germain, speak from experience. I speak as a Master because I have gone through this myself. All these grand gifts that I have – my magnificent capabilities, my ability to literally manifest grand abundance, to manifest a physical body, to be a grand lover, to have an intellect beyond all – these are not things that were given to me or bestowed upon me. I did not bargain for my gifts, I did not sell my soul to gain them. *I learned to trust myself.*

It took me many lifetimes. It took me a hundred thousand years of being in my own prison, my own crystal. It took all of these things, but it doesn't need to take you that at this point. Being a Master comes down to one thing: *Trusting yourself.*

We're going to come back to this later in our book but now let's talk about some of the attributes of the New Energy Master. Some of these attributes may seem a bit conflicting. Some of these attributes may cause you a bit of anger for they may go against things you've learned before. Allow yourself to feel those energies. Don't just accept what I say, trust what you are feeling within.

ELEGANTLY SIMPLE

The first phase of experiencing mastery, achieved through the total trust in self is this: The Master learns that *everything is elegantly simple*. This is the number one thing that you will discover – that everything is elegantly simple. Through your eyes of mistrust your view the world as being very complex and you've led yourself to believe that there is no way you are ever going to really understand how life works. Many of you have led yourself to believe that the answer will not present itself until after your physical death – which, by the way, it doesn't. But to the Master the answer can present itself *now*.

Everything is elegantly simple, it only appears complex. You are looking at this beautiful tapestry called Life from the underside of the loom where things appear to be in chaos. But as you come to a place of pure and implicit trust you will begin to see the weaving from the top. Then you will see how beautifully and simply it is laid out.

You see, energy is *just energy*. It is in a neutral state until it is charged or polarized and brought into reality. The core of everything, other than the soul, is just energy. It's not good, it's not bad; it's not organized and it's not chaos. *It is just energy*.

Your students will also be seeking the elegantly simple answers. But when you go down the intellectual and complex path you will never find the end because now you are having far too much fun on your search, going down little roads and pathways, going off on mental diversions, playing this whole game of hide and seek with yourself. But the answer is always elegantly simple.

When you are faced with situations in your own life, or when your students come to you for answers, the answers will be amazingly simple – if you let them be. Humans, by their training, try to make everything very complex, very analytical and very structured. But you see, in the scheme of all energy nothing is structured. You like to believe it is, you like to believe there are mathematical principles that define the universe, but there are not. Yes, there are illusions of it but there are also delusions of it. At its core, *everything* is elegantly simple.

Now you're saying "Well, tell me what 'simple' means," but this is for *you* to discover. With *any* situation that comes your way look beyond the complexity because the situation is simply disguised as being complex. Look into the simplicity, look into the core energy of everything around you.

If you're doing it through your mind you're probably going to complicate it. The simple answers come from the heart. The mind will follow, it will respond, it will come to its intellectual understanding as appropriate, but the Master understands that everything is elegantly simple. Sometimes the simplicity doesn't occur to you right away and that's when the mind tries to fill in, tries to find the answer by looking at the complexity rather than the simplicity.

This is the time to stop . . . take a breath . . . stop trying to force the answer . . . and allow the simple answer to come to you. It will. It always does. This is part of the magic of mastery in the New Energy. The answer *will* come to you – it has to. You have called it, you have summoned it to you, and therefore it will come. Perhaps not in that minute of time but it will come to you. It will. It is. It just is. It's not a law, it's not a principle, it just is.

I have to remind you here that, as a souled being, as a unique entity and expression of What Cannot Be Spoken, you are not an energy Being at all. Your core essence contains no energy whatsoever. You have been led to believe you're an energetic being but you are not. You *use* energy, you bring it into your reality and use it, therefore you have led yourself to believe that you *are* energy, but you're not. You are no more an energy Being than you are in this "reality" because this reality is also an illusion. You bring in energy, you use it, you let it serve you, but you are not an energy Being and that is a simple – an elegantly simple – understanding!

SELF FIRST

Do it for yourself first. This goes against the grain of many of the teachings of the past five thousand years and more. So many of the old Masters did it for everyone else. They sacrificed themselves – at least that's how the stories were written. But I can tell you of many cases where these Masters' primary concern was *not* serving others. That is a joke. That is control. How can you be a Master, how can you be a teacher if you're not taking care of yourself? This is a very simple principle.

You have been led to believe that salvation comes through serving others, by doing things like giving abundance to churches or organizations, by sacrificing yourself. That is, quite frankly, very old energy.

As a Master you take care of yourself first – your body, your mind, your spirit. You get yourself re-balanced. You get yourself clear and healthy. You get yourself working in a multi-dimensional modality. You see, most humans just exist in one – they barely exist in the third dimension. But you are now going to be existing in multiple dimensions.

When you are clear, balanced and healthy, others will see and feel that. You will become the Standard for them. If you are broken down, if you are sick, if you are financially exhausted and running from the bill collectors, this is going to set no example for others and it will essentially make your mastery a joke. Others humans need to see an example of mastery and, more than anything, *you deserve it.*

Can you accept that? You deserve it. You deserve to take care of yourself. You see, being out of trust with yourself you have been led to believe that you shouldn't take care of yourself. You have been led to believe that you must do it for everyone else, not yourself.

These words were developed: "Selfish;" "egotistical;" "full of yourself;" and they are seen as a bad thing. But I say to you it is the grandest thing to be self-full! I can serve and help and teach others only when I am clear and balanced. You hear me, in my own braggadocios way, talking of my own grandness and intellect – and my charm of course, my good looks – in part because I am giving you an example. You see, if you can't say it about yourself first you can be sure no one else is going to say it for you.

The Master takes care of themselves first and this is going to go against most – if not all – of the training you have had and it will certainly go against the training of the students who come to you. They are going to be shocked at first, even angry, but eventually they're going to come to understand. Take care of yourself first.

Take care of yourself. It is the most profound and sacred thing you can do for you.

You do not have a responsibility to other humans, you do not have a responsibility to mass consciousness, and it's time to realize that this whole idea that everyone has to move forward at the same time is also an illusion. There are some who teach and preach that what happens to one happens to all, that if there is one straggler then all must wait but that is not true at all. You are each sovereign. There is nothing that says you have to fix or repair anyone else and in fact that is a dishonor to them.

The greatest thing you can do for others is honor them for their path, for their choices – no matter what – and the second greatest thing you can do for them is to be there when they call out for a teacher. But don't try to teach the ones who aren't asking for a teacher. You have seen what has happened with the churches and their evangelistic movements, how they try to convert everyone. Has it brought peace to the earth? Has it fed the poor? Has it solved the world's problems to inflict your will and your dream on others? Absolutely not. If humans were taught to have respect and compassion for every other human, no matter where they were, *that* would truly change the energy.

Take care of yourself first. It's a very important principle.

Let's take a deep breath.

ALL ENERGY SERVES

The Master understands that all energies serve them. Again, this goes against the grain of most of the teachings of the past. Energy wants to serve you, that's why it's there. In fact, you put it there to serve you at the appropriate time.

Energy exists in a wide variety of different types of what you would call locations. It is stored in various different types of cosmic or angelic reservoirs, including this thing called the Field, which is simply neutral energy waiting to serve you.

There is energy within you, waiting to serve you. There are non-physical entities, at your feet right now, waiting to serve you. Your pets are waiting to serve you. Opportunities, new jobs, waiting to serve you. Money, waiting to serve you. They are all in line waiting to serve you but you have your back turned for you have been led to believe that you must serve everyone and everything else. You have even been led to believe that the word "servant" is negative – and it's not.

The Master understands this pure principle. The Master understands that they will never own the energy – because you *own* nothing at all. But the Master understands that all energy wants to serve them and they honor that.

It could be another person who suddenly appears in your life, wanting to do something for you. How often do you push this type of thing out of your life because you don't feel you're worthy? Or because you feel you have to do it yourself in the old struggling way? Or because you're afraid that they have an agenda?

The energy of money is here to serve you, but humans have this belief system that money is evil. Well, I wonder who taught you that? Other humans, other institutions, even churches. Money is nothing but a piece of paper. You are led to believe that it has worth and value, so therefore it does and it's here to serve you. It wants to come into your life.

There are devas, nature beings, who want to serve you when you go out for a walk in the woods, but you pretend that they're not there, pretend you don't understand how they can serve you. You pretend that you need more enlightenment before anything like that could ever happen to you. But actually these Beings are here on earth in service to you and in service to Gaia. *Let* them serve you for this gives them great satisfaction. It is why they are here right now. It is part of their evolution to be in that kind of service. It gives them fulfillment and it certainly brings them joy to serve you.

The angelic beings all around you, we are in service. We are lined up waiting. Many of you have had the old concept of spirit guides and you tried to use them to do things *for* you, to answer your questions, to lead you. But that's not why they're here. They are here to be in service and to go to work for you when you make choices and as you become Masters.

The Master understands that all energy serves them. Use it. Play with it. Bring it into your life. Don't be embarrassed if another person, another Being comes to serve you. You are the Master, accept that position.

No Compromise

The Master does not compromise. The Master does not compromise their values and, more than anything, they don't compromise their trust. We're not talking so much about interpersonal relationships here. We're not saying that you can't work things out with another person in a cooperative way. We're talking about not compromising your own core values, your own core trust.

Many times humans will compromise what they believe in because they don't trust themselves, they're actually unsure. They will compromise their simplicity, their integrity and what they know to be right for themselves. And when you compromise who you know you are, you just fall more and more out of trust with yourself.

Now this has nothing to do with working with other people. This has to do with you and your own Self. When you are in a situation that's calling for you to compromise, go back to *your* values, back to *yourself.* Humans compromise themselves in so many situations instead of following what they know to be real, what they know to be right. This is the time to take a deep breath and look at what is happening. Every time you compromise yourself and your own values, in a sense it is like splitting yourself in pieces, cutting yourself into small fragments so you're no longer whole and complete. Then you are a series of compromised and mistrusting fragments or aspects of yourself.

The Master stays true to themselves. They do not compromise.

CHOICE

The Master makes choices. Now that seems to be fairly obvious but when you look at the reality of the human condition you realize that most humans really don't make choices. Oh, they make little choices about what to wear that day but even then they are terribly confused! It is so aggravating for those of us in these other realms to watch you try to get up in the morning. You go through all this confusion and we have to shake our heads and say "This is going to be a difficult day! If they can't make a choice about what to wear or what to eat for breakfast, we're going to have a long day with this human entity."

The Master makes choices and *is not afraid of them.* So many humans are afraid to make a choice because they are afraid they're going to make the wrong choice, afraid they're going to make a choice that upsets somebody else, afraid to make a choice that would cause ripples in the matrix. They are afraid to do anything that makes them stand out or look different. They have essentially been programmed *not* to make choices but just to follow the path of everyone else.

The Master makes very specific choices because this is what a Master and a Creator does. The Master also understands that, when making choices, they never own the outcome. They never limit or control the outcome for a choice is simply a direction and a potential which they allow to unfold. It is yours but you give it freedom and allow it to unfold in an unrestricted way.

When you make a deliberate and conscious choice in your life you change your energetic dynamic. You change the way you bring energy into your life and the way you send out energy into your life. When you make a conscious and deliberate choice, you energize yourself. You put a type of charge or movement on the energy. However, when you are not making choices, there is no movement and if there is no movement you cannot bring the appropriate things into your life.

So the Master makes choices – high level choices. The Master makes choices to be abundant; choices to be the Master; choices to be the Teacher; choices to be balanced in biology and physiology.

These are the types of choices a Master makes, not necessarily what shoes to wear. However, you will find that as you make the high level choices in your life everything below starts to fill in. You won't have to stand at your closet, trying to figure out what to wear because you will know who you are and you will understand how to reflect that in your clothing. You won't have to stand at your closet each day deciding if you're colorful, if you're drab, if you're casual, if you're formal. You will pick the exact right thing because it is a reflection of you. You won't have to stand in front of the mirror in the morning wondering if how you look is appropriate because you know you will look superb. You are the reflection of your choices.

Make choices. High level choices. The smaller choices tend to fill themselves in. Making choices is a bold step. You're going to be surprised after this about how you have not been making choices and you're going to become very clear in watching other humans going about their lives, how they truly make no choices. They follow in their ruts. That is a choice, I guess, but not a choice that a Master would make.

SELF CONTAINMENT

A Master understands that they are a self-contained Being. You do not need to get one particle or one morsel of energy from anywhere outside of you. As a Master you are self-contained. You are like a perpetual energy machine. You don't need to get energy from the outside and you don't need to give out energy either. You are self-contained. Everything you need is within you.

This is something the Masters of the past could not do. However the Masters of the New Energy can because there has been a shift, since late 2005, that you have allowed to take place at a deep level within you. You have brought your own energy machine into this reality, brought it literally into the physical body. It works within all of the cells and the atoms and the blank spaces in your physical body to supply you with all of the energy that you need.

Perhaps you ask, "Then why do I need to eat food?" Ultimately you will actually be able to *not* eat food. You will be able to self-generate the energy. You don't need to get energy from anywhere else, particularly other people. You don't need to feed off of them. You don't need anything that they have. You don't even need to derive energy from this thing that we call the Field – although you are welcome to do it by choice. But you don't need it because you are totally self-contained.

This seems like a basic principle, but humans have been trained to believe that everything comes from outside of them. Everything. They have been taught that they have to learn it on the outside, acquire it on the outside, beg for it on the outside or pray for it on the outside. The truth is that you already have it but you don't trust yourself, so you haven't been using it. You don't trust that it's really there. You don't even trust these words I'm saying to you. You think I'm talking to someone else. You *do* have it. Start to use it. Start to play with it. Start to experience what it is like to be your own energy generator.

When I talk about energy I'm talking about energy to sustain your physical body, energy to keep your mind going *and* tapped into the Universal Consciousness. Energy to sustain your spirit here on earth – that in itself is monumental. Until recently it was very difficult to sustain your spirit or your essence or your soul here in this reality. It was off somewhere else, essentially in a type of cocoon, taking an inward look on another dimensional realm. But slowly, surely, you have been creating the space, you have been creating the type of principle or dynamic that now allows the melding back together of your essence into this reality and into this Now moment.

You can't dissect your body and find where this essence resides because it is in everything. It doesn't exist in a certain energy band around you, it's not hidden in a chakra. It *is* you and now you have access to that – to you, yourself, your spirit, your soul, whatever you want to call it – in this reality, right here and now.

You are a self-contained energy Being and you are the first generation of Masters who have ever had that.

MORE ON TRUST

Take a deep breath.
Breathe in trust in yourself.

Perhaps is has been a long time since you've experienced what it is like to truly trust you – your feelings, your intuitions, your own guidance, your own personal leadership within yourself. Perhaps it has been too long since you have allowed yourself to move beyond all of the doubts, beyond all those limitations to truly trust yourself.

When you first start allowing this trust to come in you're going to be looking for certain signs and I am going to ask you to actually overlook those instead. As you get back into the practice of trusting yourself you're going to want to know that you are doing the right thing, making the right choice. You'll want to know you are right. But here and now, when it comes to trusting yourself, I'm going to ask you to let go of that concept of right and wrong.

I know it can be a little frightening, because part of your whole system of defense – which is designed to protect you, your physical body, your mind, and all these different parts of you – is based on knowing what is right and wrong. And, when you open up to trusting yourself, the fear comes up that perhaps you're going to overstep yourself and do the wrong thing.

However, there is a self-correcting or self-adjusting process that takes place. As you begin to open up to trust, open up to your own feelings, you're not always going to come up with what you, in your human self, would call the "right answers." But then that would lead us to a whole discussion about what is right and what is not. Right and wrong are perceptions, that is all. They are simply perceptions. Perhaps you say "But if I trust myself and then my body becomes hurt and I'm in pain, was that not the wrong thing?" Not necessarily. Also, you are interjecting fear into this whole concept of returning to trust in yourself, almost to throw yourself off track. As you return to self trust you are going to find that your life has so much more depth, that you have so many more capabilities than you have allowed or been open to in the past.

When you open up to trust it can also be a bit frightening because, at first, it's going to feel lonely. You are very accustomed to going outside of yourself for trust, looking to other people, other authorities, other entities. So at first it can feel cold, alone, and a bit frightening, but that is just part of the initial process. As you work with trust, just like you work with the breath, you learn to get past that initial fear or resistance. You learn that the answers that come from within you have so much more depth and meaning. Life itself will return to a point of meaning and understanding and in every moment it will have this elegant simplicity that I talked about earlier.

Illusion

The Master understands that life is an illusion. In the first segment I spoke about the importance of trust, how it is the way of the Master of the New Energy. As you trust yourself you begin to discover things about yourself that relate to you within yourself, but then the outside world and how you interact with it starts changing as well.

You are living in a very real illusion, you and everyone in the world around you. Now I know that just the term "illusion" makes it sound almost invalid, but it is a very real illusion and it is very valid. *It is actually the manifestation of your beliefs, your desires and your choices.* It is all around you – but it is also an illusion. At times you get so caught up in the reality of this illusion that you come to believe that it is inflexible, that it cannot be moved, shifted and changed. *But it is an illusion* and therefore it can be shifted, changed, expanded – anything – at anytime.

What you are seeing outside of you is simply the reflection of the internal relationship between yourself and you, as well as the relationship between yourself and the outside world. We're going to get into some of the magic of this later on but for now understand that it is *all* an illusion. Therefore, you are not locked into it. It can change – and be changed – at any time.

ACCEPTANCE

The Master learns to accept all things as they are. Again this sounds very simple – and it is – but there are many, many facets of this truth.

So many humans try to change other people to conform with their own views and beliefs. They try to change the outside world to make it the way they think or feel it should be. The result of this is continual conflict within themselves because the outside world doesn't necessarily respond and then they are always disappointed by what's going on outside of them. But as Shaumbra, you learned early on to *accept all things as they are.*

This is, by the way, the ultimate compassion – to accept and honor all things and people *as they are.* As you do this, you discover that there is no more conflict, there is no more collision. You find that life – your life and your creations – take on a new kind of ease.

As you accept all things exactly as they are you also begin to understand that they are in their own state of perfection. This won't just be an intellectual concept for you. We know some of you have heard the words "All things are in perfection," but to really feel it and to really experience this is a true blessing. Your job here on earth is not to try to force change on the world. You came here to be teachers for those who choose change within themselves.

This is one of the most important principles of mastery and one that many humans find difficult to grasp. They are discontent with the world around them but the real truth is that they are discontent with themselves.

This is a very important principle for you, for your students, and actually for all of humanity: to accept all that is *as it is*, even the most difficult things, the most challenging experiences. If you see a beggar on the street corner, to accept that. If you see someone who is physically handicapped, to understand that they have chosen that. It is for you to honor and accept all things as they are. The Master understands and lives by this principle.

THE UNKNOWN

The Master allows themselves to experience – truly experience – what is called the Unknown or the Unsaid. You have this concept of God, of Spirit, and it is a concept that has now, with religions and belief systems, become very diluted and very human-like. In the truest sense, you cannot say or define Spirit.

In some of the old religious documents it is called the "Unknown" or the "Four Words That Cannot Be Said," and many interpreted this to mean that one was not allowed to utter the words or the name of God. But what was really meant is that there is no way for the human to actually understand or try to define God or Spirit. It just is. You could spend lifetimes trying to write about what Spirit is, what God is, what Jehovah is. You could try to define it to another person but then it's just your own concept coming from the human mind. *It just is.*

The Master learns to not to try to define this thing, this name that cannot even be said, but rather to *experience* it in their life. *It is you.* It is within you. It is within all things as well, but more than anything it is uniquely within *you.*

To experience What Cannot Be Said, to experience this Spirit – and we don't even like to use that word – requires utmost trust in yourself. To allow that essence of your own God Self to come through requires total and implicit trust in Self. It is a God Self that you're not trying to define, you're not trying to label, you're not trying to put into human terms. It is a pure and simple experience.

Let's take a moment here, in this very safe space, to not think about what God is or isn't; to not even try to put your mental arms around terms like "omnipotent" or "omnipresent" or any of these other things; and just be so trusting in yourself that you can just experience it.

Let's take a moment now...

Take a deep breath...

(long pause)

The Master understands that they are experiencing it right now. It is only the human who says "But I feel nothing. I'm experiencing nothing. I expected lightning bolts, or the lights to flicker, or maybe a voice in my head." Oh Shaumbra, that is when you try to make it so complex and try to define it in your human terms, when you think you need to have something like drama or something that touches your current human senses.

But you are experiencing what cannot be said or defined. You are experiencing this grandness of Spirit right now. For a brief moment you let this Essence of all essences come right into your body, come right into your mind, into your soul. And you see, it doesn't need to yell or scream, it doesn't need to create some sort of dramatic impact, it doesn't need to make your body hot or cold. *It just is.*

Humans have been searching for this complex or dramatic type of God for a long time. They have been searching for some outside Being who is going to come in and solve all of their problems. But they will never find this God.

The Master understands that the experience of the Unknown, the Unsaid, is always there. It is a deep and still pool. It is calm. It is quiet. It doesn't carry the attributes that you would typically associate with any human behavior or human identity. It is so pure that it goes unnoticed by all but the true Master. The Master understands that it simply *is*. And the Master understands that experiencing it means simply allowing it into their reality, participating with it with no expectations.

Sometimes humans want to measure energies or experiences, they want to try to define them in certain ways. But the Master allows themselves to experience the Unknown deep within them, without needing to define it.

Take a deep breath now...

And allow yourself to experience What Cannot Be Said.

(long pause)

The essence of your own Spirit is looking for a relationship with you in this reality. Oh, it has always been there, always been available to you, but it has been kept in other realities. It has been kept out of this human condition. Now, in this moment, it is looking for that relationship with you here in this reality. But it will be difficult to identify if you use the old means of trying to understand it.

Your Spirit truly, truly begs you to open up, to expand your energy and go beyond how you have understood or interpreted energies in the past. It truly asks you to go beyond. Beyond the mind, beyond your current sensory perceptions.

As you allow yourself to experience this Unknown, this Spirit, it will start becoming very known to you, again in ways that you will probably never be able to define in words. You will try to explain it to a friend, even to another Shaumbra, and you will seem to get all jumbled in your words because *it just is*. That is why the ancient ones said it is the Name That Cannot Be Said. It is the Expression That Cannot Be Defined. We don't even want to use the word Spirit, for it goes beyond that and the Master understands this. The Master allows themselves to experience this Unknown every moment of every day.

FACETS AND LAYERS

The Master explores all facets of energies. Lets begin by talking about a very inanimate object such as a rock, a stone. It has many facets, many layers of energy. The focus of human consciousness would be on the rock itself – that it is hard, that it comes from the earth and that it is not living. But the Master understands there is much, much more to this rock.

This rock has consciousness. It doesn't necessarily have a soul or a spirit like you do but it is conscious and aware of itself as a rock. That's why it has a particular size, shape and density. It has its own awareness of itself. Now if that rock was smashed into two, it would still have the awareness of itself from when it was whole but now also as two separate pieces.

The rock has consciousness of the water as well. It has an awareness and remembrance of every drop of rain that has ever fallen upon it, every ocean or river that it has ever bathed. It is at a different layer or level than the actual hard rock that you perceive, but it is there.

The Master understands that. The Master is not fooled by the physical identity that is perceived through the human senses of sight, touch, taste, sound or smell. The Master understands that they can travel to all of these layers and levels within something as simple as a rock. The Master can allow themselves to go to the facets of that rock that have been touched by a drop of water and connect back, through that drop of water, to every other object that that drop of water has ever fallen upon. Through that drop of water the Master can connect to everything else, not just from the past few years but from the creation of earth and from the time water started falling from the clouds.

You can journey back through that single drop of water to the day that it touched you in a past life, to when you drank that drop of water and it flowed through your body. You can connect to an aspect of yourself from the past just through that facet of the rock that was touched by that drop of water.

Through that drop of water, which is connected to all of the other drops of water in all of the oceans and the seas of the world, you can connect to the aquatic life, to the animal world. You can connect back to the grand Masters. You can connect back to the cup of water that Buddha drank when he was sitting under the tree. You can experience with Buddha what it was like during his time of enlightenment, just through that rock. Now, if that rock contains so many facets and layers and levels, then everything else does as well.

Humans take for granted what they see with their eyes and feel with their hands but they are looking at life in a very limited way and through a very narrow spectrum. The Master understands that everything in life – every object, every experience, every emotion – has many, many facets, many, many layers.

When you are talking with another human allow yourself to travel the layers within them and you will see that they are comprised of many layers, that they also have many facets. If you are a healer or one who does energy work, go beyond just the person you see in front of you. Look at their other layers and levels. Look at what is motivating them in the background. Pay attention not only to the words they are telling you but to all of their layers and levels.

When you are reading a book, for instance, there are layers and levels within it, including this one. It is not just the words that are printed upon the pages, there are also the layers and levels of every one of the voices and every one of the experiences of the Masters who added their energy to help write this book. It includes not only the experiences of each of them in this lifetime but going back many, many lifetimes as well.

From any single point, from any single object, you can connect to its other layers and levels, its facets. And from those facets you can journey back through time, through and across space, and connect with anything else – and not just on this earth. You can connect from any object – even a bottle of soda – and connect through that into the other realms. Perhaps you sometimes get confused and lost when you try to open up multi-dimensionally. Try doing it now through a single object. The Master understands that everything – every object, every experience, every emotion, everything – has many facets. Again, this sounds like a simple principle but humans live in a very narrow, very singular type of existence. They don't allow themselves to experience the unknown. They don't allow themselves to open up to all of these different facets that are right here. As you work with your students take them through simple exercises to help them understand that *everything*, even a rock, is multidimensional.

No Expectations

The Master understands that they are the creator but allows the outcome of everything to be open. In other words, if you decide to create grand health for yourself in this lifetime, you are making a choice now. You are creating. You are setting up an energetic charge that is heard by your body. There is something called Standard Technology where one perfect, healthy cell can radiate out your creation, your choice for health, to every other cell, and it can begin to re-balance your body. *But don't limit the outcome.* Don't just focus on getting over that pain you have in your leg, or making your heart stronger. Allow your creations to be very open ended.

Perhaps you are considering starting a business. You have been contemplating it for a while and now you are making a choice to begin. You are making a choice which then starts the energy moving and aligning itself towards your choice. But the moment you put a limitation on it, the moment you have an expectation of the outcome, you start to restrict it again. You start de-charging yourself and your creation. You start shifting and changing how energies will be brought to you.

This is one thing that is very, very common for humans, particularly those who are on the metaphysical path. They get into this whole area of conscious creation and they find that it is an exciting new tool. But then they also use limitation or too much definition. They create at one point, but they limit the result at another through definition and expectation of what it should be.

True creation is open-ended. It flows. As your creation starts to take on its own life it starts accumulating or bringing in other energies as well and the very nature of your original choice, your original creation, can far surpass what you ever imagined it could be. When you place an expectation or a limitation on it, or you have a belief that it will be limited, you will definitely limit the outcome.

Let go of all expectation of the results. Let go of what you think it should look like or how it should act. Use the simple, conscious creation – the choice – and then watch how the energy evolves and expands. There is no need to control it, there is no need to limit it. Just allow it to evolve and expand. It is still yours but now it has taken on its own life, its own energy, its own dynamic.

Now you, as its original creator, can collapse it at any time. If you say that you are no longer happy with this creation, you no longer want it to be in your energy or your consciousness, you can collapse it. So you never have to worry that it's going to get out of hand. But, while it is dynamic, while it is living, allow it to be open ended. You're going to find this is a much more pleasant and rewarding way of creating.

No Force

The Master understands that it is about flow, not force. You live in a world of duality. You have the elements of negative and positive, masculine and feminine, right and wrong, up and down – all of these aspects of duality. That is how you come into this life and that is how you exist throughout this life. Humans are conditioned to believe that, in order to get through life, they must use force. If you want something to happen you have to force it, you have to push to get it done or force your energy on other people to get it done. So life is always about struggling, always about pushing. Most humans feel they are pushing large flat stones uphill because that is what it takes to exist in the current energy of duality.

The Master understands that there is truly no force needed. The Master understands that it is all about flow. This is somewhat of a difficult concept because you are so used to using force, having to *make* it happen. How about *allowing* it to happen?

In the New Energy you literally become an energetic attraction point to your choices and your creations. You become like a magnet where you draw towards you and into you all the energies that are waiting to serve you, all the energies that are needed to support what you are doing. This attraction is a flow, not a force.

Look at things in your life. If you are having to force them, if they are a struggle, either you are not using conscious choice, not trusting yourself as a creator; or you are getting caught up in this whole Old Energy paradigm of force. Force does work, by the way, as you have found out. You can force certain things to happen. By pushing hard, by demanding, by using your own personal energy as a type of battering ram, you *can* make things happen. And then you say "See? Saint-Germain was wrong. Force does work." Yes it does, up to a point.

Every time you force something in this three-dimensional reality, there is always an opposing force, here or somewhere else, that comes into play for that is how energy works. It always balances itself. Energy always seeks resolution so if there is a force at one level there will be a counter-force at another level.

This doesn't necessarily mean it's going to come in and slap you on the backside or come in and play some sort of karma on you. But somewhere, at some reality or dimensional level, there will be a counter-force. There has to be. And sooner or later you're going to encounter or experience that counter-force. It might be days later or weeks later. It might be in what you would consider to be a totally unrelated episode in your life. It could even be between lifetimes where you go to explore the counter-force of every force that you've ever used. Force does work but there's always the reverse, there's always the backside, always the balance.

In the New Energy there is a flow of energy. There is a flow of consciousness. There is a flow of energies aligning to meet and to serve your creations. The flow is easy, natural, very simple and very elegant. Things just seem to happen – without stress, without force – so much so that you might not be used to it or satisfied with it because you are used to having a reaction every time you try to make something happen.

Let's say you're trying to start your business. You are only satisfied when you feel like you've done something that day. But what you're doing is simply measuring the amount of force that went out, not the creation that might have taken place. It is a type of delusion – or illusion – that the amount of effort you put out has anything to do with the result.

There is a natural flow that takes place and this flow doesn't necessarily cause drama or reaction. Things just happen. They just turn into a coincidence because, in this flow, they synchronize with all of the other elements. Sometimes there is a propensity in the human to feel that maybe they didn't do enough to make something happen, that they didn't struggle enough, didn't sweat enough. It's time to get over that.

You will find, as you allow this flow into your creations and into your life, that it frees up so much of your energy and time to do things that are truly joyful, things that you truly have passion to do.

We have talked elsewhere about soul passion. Perhaps you have been searching for it for a long time, wondering "What is my soul passion? Where is my soul passion? Why isn't it in my life?" Well, it is, but you are so preoccupied with trying to make things happen, your energy is so consumed with the ongoing daily struggles with force and counter-force, that it occupies all of your energy. There is nothing left to truly go in and explore and experience your own soul passion. The soul passion is there, it is waiting in the wings for when you to have the time and the energy to invite it into your life. But if you're so caught up in the old duality way of creating – force on force – your soul passion is going to continue to wait until you give it the opening or the opportunity to come in.

Take a deep breath now and allow yourself now to experience the *flow* versus the *force*.

(pause)

You see, the flow is subtle. It doesn't contain drama, it doesn't contain highs and lows. There are no opposing energies in it because the energies have lined up. They are coming in to serve you rather than oppose each other – which was the reason for duality in the first place.

Let us take, for instance, what you call light and dark: The reason for having these two elements was so they could be mirrors or reflections of each other. By constantly battling or colliding they eventually come to a better understanding of themselves. But sooner or later they get tired of this constant colliding and their energies meld back together. That is what is happening in this new era and that is what you, as Masters, can tap into.

CREATION

The Master understands that they are a creator. It is a very simple concept, you have heard it before, but now it's time to start putting it to use. The Master understands that they are the creator. *You* are the point of creation – right here, right now – and when you make a choice you start the creation process happening.

It doesn't come from anywhere or anyone else. You don't need to have supernatural powers. Creation happens the moment you choose to create and then it begins expressing itself. Your creation expresses itself through you. It lines up all of the energies within you, it draws in energies from outside of you that want to come into your reality, and then it begins unfolding. That is when you begin to experience the magic. That is when you begin to see how true creation opens and flows.

Actually at some point it might get a little frightening because you're going to find out how easy it is to create, especially when you don't have limitations on the outcome. When you're using flow energy instead of duality energy, it just starts happening and there's going to come a point where you get a bit intimidated by your own creation ability. You'll think "If it's this easy, perhaps I'm such a grand creator that I can destroy the whole world!" Actually you probably could with the energies that you have – but you won't because of the wisdom that you also have.

You are at a point right now where you are far too wise to misuse energies. You're not going to want to harm other people or blow up the world or take advantage of others. You have come too far and gained too much wisdom for things like that. But there is still a part of you that doesn't trust, so you hold back. However, when you allow your trust to come through you will realize that you will always use your creation abilities wisely.

By the way, a creator is a *creator* not an *imitator*. There is a big difference between creating and imitating. Imitations are very, very limited because you are taking a concept that was already created and you're trying to duplicate it. It's not going to be any bigger than the original, in fact it will be quite a lot smaller. The creator starts with something from within themselves – their own idea, their own desire. Yes, they may relate it to other things but when they truly initiate and launch the creation it is theirs. They are not imitating anyone else.

The Master understands that they are the creator and they take responsibility for it. They don't give the responsibility to the angels or to God. They take full responsibility for it in that moment.

Take a deep breath now and feel that energy of you, the creator.

I know you may doubt this. You still have yet to see how you are a creator, how you are making this happen. But it is very simple and it is very, very easy.

DISCERNMENT

The Master understands their own discernment. Quite simply, the Master understands *what is theirs and what is not.* Because of the interconnection of energy, particularly the interconnection of consciousness between all humans and all things, it is very easy to get caught into the confusion about what is yours and what is not. So often you accept energies that aren't yours at all. You take them in but it is like taking in the homeless. You give them a place to live, you give them a refuge from the outside, but so often they start to take your energy – and they are not your responsibility.

Many of you claim thoughts, feelings and energies that are not yours. Some of the physical pains that you have are not yours. You are actually carrying somebody else's physical pain, it is not yours but you pretend it is. Perhaps you carry it because of some ancestral karma. Perhaps it is something in your family line that has been passed down from one to the other and now you carry it. *It is not yours* and it actually doesn't look very good on you.

Perhaps you are simply carrying mass consciousness energy, feeling the energies of this general anxiety of humanity. Perhaps you are carrying around deep depression that doesn't belong to you. You may have inherited it from an aspect of yourself in a past life – a very depressed aspect – who is still hanging around you, but now you believe it's yours just like you believe your past life is yours. It's not. It is an aspect, an expression of your energy, *but it is not you.* You are different in this lifetime. You are sovereign in this lifetime. You have a connection to your past lifetimes but they are not you and you are not them.

Perhaps you are carrying energies of the place where you work. Step back for a moment from your office, this place you work, both the physical place and the energetic place. It has an energy, and if you step back far enough you can perceive it. When you're there on a day-to-day level it's very hard to discern the energy, but step back. Some workplaces have a very harsh, strict, intense energy. Others have a very struggling energy. Ask yourself "What position is this company in right now? Is it struggling against its competitors? Is it having financial issues? Environmental issues? Staff issues?" Step back and *feel* the energy of your office.

Now, take a look at yourself. Are you having similar types of issues in your life? Are you carrying the energies of your office within yourself? There's a very good chance you are. You also do it with your family and your friends. You even do it with Shaumbra because you are so connected with them. This connection is wonderful but you sometimes tend to take on the physical symptoms of other Shaumbra. Stand back, as Tobias says, behind the short wall. Which of these energies are yours and which are not? The Master is a Master of discernment. What is yours? What belongs outside of you?

You tend to take on other people's issues. You don't need to – and a Master doesn't want to – because you can't do things to get these energies moving again. You can't help others resolve their issues if you're caught right in the middle of it. You take on the baggage, problems and energies of others, thinking that you're doing some type of sacrificial service, that you're somehow saving the world. *You're not.* You are only burdening yourself and then you get frustrated because things aren't working out better for you.

Step back. Which of those energies do you *choose* to continue holding onto? First of all, discern which are truly yours and which are not. Then, *choose* which of those energies you are ready to let go of. And then take a look at why you have been keeping them. What would have made you want to own them in the first place?

Some of you are going to feel a bit barren and unfulfilled by not carrying around the woes of the world because you have been hypnotized into thinking that this is your responsibility. You have come to believe that this is what you have to do as a "good person." I'll tell you right now, the true Masters of the past – and of the present – understand that they are not being effective by just carrying around all of these burdens. They are much more effective being a balanced, centered and complete Master within themselves. It is much easier to give advice to other humans when you are coming from a place of integration and balance.

This is a sticky one. It's sticky because it's sticking on you and you have difficulty seeing it. Perhaps you think I'm talking to someone else but I'm going to ask you to explore this within yourself. What are your energies – your own true energies – and what belong somewhere else?

Anything you choose not to be yours is no longer yours. You think "Oh, but I have earned this, I was a bad person at some point in my life or I did something wrong, or..." See? You are so bought into it that you find all these ways to justify it being yours. The Master is discerning and understands they can release anything they choose. Conflicts going on inside yourself, whether physical or mental – you can let them go. Beliefs, feelings, reactions – any of those. Whatever you *choose* is yours. Anything else, let it go.

Perhaps you are afraid to let it go because you think you're going to pollute the energy or the consciousness of the world if you let it go, much like a smoke stack would pollute it with smoke going back out into the air. You won't. When you release something that you no longer choose, you take the charge off of it and it simply reverts back to its pure and natural state of energy – which is neutral but filled with potential. It's not like you're passing some sort of bad energetic gas and everybody else is going to smell it! You release it back into purity, back into simplicity and back into neutrality.

The Master is very discerning about *what is theirs and what is not.*

GRANDNESS

The Master understands that they create from the full Self and not just from the limited human need self. That's a mouthful! What this means is that so often your simple human needs dictate and rule your life. The need for food, clothing, shelter, affection – these very basic human needs rule your universe. However the Master understands that, as they create from the complete self, as they create from the level of total self trust, these human needs take care of themselves so easily they are almost automatic. Because you are creating from the grand scale, the soul passion level, the true desire level, it all trickles down and fills in the human needs. It satisfies you and it takes care of all those things.

Right now, your energy is preoccupied with your human needs. So often you are creating out of the desperate human need place rather than the grand magnificent soul self, full self place. Do you see the difference? Do you see that when you create on the grand scale it all filters down and fills in the human needs? It is a natural occurrence.

When you create from this very limited human desperation place, desperation energy then surrounds your creations and they are limited right from the start. You'll get a limited response to your creation energy but it won't be what you really desire.

Expand your energy beyond desperation. *Be a Master.* Create from your true and full passion, not just the desperate human self. Perhaps you are having a hard time paying your rent this month – and you're trying to create from that place? That is pathetic. You are going to have difficulties with this Mastership program if that's where you're coming from. You say, "But Saint-Germain, that is my need today! I'm going to be evicted here quite shortly, that is my need." I'm going to ask you to back away from it. That is what you *think* your need is. That is the trap that you have gotten yourself into. That is your desperation.

Desperate people do desperate things. Desperate creators make desperate creations. You get so tangled up in your issues. *Step back.* Sometimes humans are so messed up in their creations I have to say to them "It's about time you died because you've got to clear that up! Just die. We'll talk about it, then you can go back to earth and start all over." "Pick rich parents the next time," I tell them.

Shaumbra, you don't have to be at that point. Step back. Understand that you create on a grand, magnificent level. Feel the grandness right now.

Take a deep breath and feel it right now.

(pause)

Tell yourself – silently within yourself – and feel whether it's real or not: "*I am grand!*"

Does it feel real? If it doesn't, continue to feel into that layer, into that facet of yourself that is grand. Perhaps that facet is buried deep somewhere but it is there. Reconnect with that energy and *feel* your grandness. Get out of this human desperation.

When the Master creates at the grand level, rather than at the human need level, the human needs are simply taken care of. Ask some of the Masters who have contributed to this book and who have done that in their life. The human needs are incidental.

ASCENDED MASTERS

As we discussed in previous sections, being a Master in the New Energy is quite different than being a Master in the old times. The consciousness of earth right now is so very different than it was a thousand years ago, five thousand years ago, or in the time of any of your old Masters. Even those who you call the Ascended Masters – a term we don't particularly care for, by the way – but the wise Beings who have lived on earth before and who are now in the other realms, even they do not understand what it is like to go through this process of personal integration in the New Energy because they did it in a different time.

There are many books that have been written about the Ascended Masters and there is much discussion today about this wise and very elite group. But they have not gone through the process that you are going through into your own mastery. They can help you – but only up to a certain point. They can help you with some basic understandings, but at a certain point even they have to back away to allow you to go through your own process of discovery. They have to allow you to go through the door into the New Energy on your own. That is why, even though many of you have felt the guidance of the Ascended Masters in the past, in more recent years you have felt you that you lost your connection with many of them. You have felt that they were gone. It's not because they have left for they are still there. It is that you have moved forward, going beyond even where they have gone.

MORE ON ACCEPTANCE

It has been said that it is easier to fix the road than it is to fix the man. This is because the road *accepts what it is* whereas the man walking upon it does not accept himself. So it is easier to spend all of the resources and time and money to repair the road so that the broken man can walk along it.

This comes to a simple point in your journey to mastery: Acceptance. First the acceptance of yourself, which is one of the most difficult things a conscious human will ever do. A conscious human sees themselves as broken; as limited; as not being able to heal themselves, much less others; as having limitations in their mind; as having weaknesses. This has been taught to them, it is a belief system that they have adopted and it is so deep within them that they don't even recognize what they are doing to themselves. Humans don't accept who they are. They are always trying to fix something but never quite able to complete it. They always critical of themselves, always analyzing themselves, always struggling within themselves and in doing this they are consuming tremendous amounts of energy.

The Master accepts everything about themselves. They see themselves with the eyes of compassion, with the gentleness of the wind. They look at themselves as an identity but not as that identity being all of who they truly are.

Take a moment here, in this safe energy, to look at yourself. Can you accept *all* that you are? Your age, can you accept that? This is something I know many humans struggle with. You feel you are getting into the second half of your life and you're struggling against your age – which does nothing other than to make the age stand out even more.

Your height, your weight, your physical appearance – can you accept these as they are? Can you accept this body that you are within, unconditionally? Lovingly? Can you accept it without any ifs or buts? Without saying "I can accept it as soon as I lose weight, as soon as I start working out, as soon as I do something to fix it"? Because that is a carrot that you will never be able to eat. You will always hold something out in front of you, thereby denying yourself the pleasure and the satisfaction of physical self-acceptance.

Perhaps you have had physical issues in your body and you're running from those, trying to cover them up, trying to ignore them. These physical symptoms that come up – whether it is problems in the stomach, the heart, or simply aches and pains – these are just signs to you that something needs attention. Something needs your love and your acceptance.

Can you totally accept your body, *as it is right now*, unconditionally? Can you accept your mind? Your thoughts? You see, when thoughts are not accepted, when you don't acknowledge them, they come back in a different way, stronger, bigger, more monstrous than ever. Because, again, this is something within you that needs your attention, your love and your acceptance.

Self-acceptance is perhaps the most difficult and challenging thing you will ever face. Not only is it difficult for you to look at yourself with acceptance, but everything you're getting from outside of you – from other people, from the outside world – is simply mirroring and reflecting how you feel about yourself. If you do not love and accept who you are, this is going to show up to you through the other humans that you come in contact with and it's going to reinforce your non-acceptance. Why should you accept yourself when others don't? When they don't listen to you, when they don't respect and honor you, when they abuse you, why should you give these things to yourself? This issue of self- acceptance is so simple, so elegant, but yet so difficult.

The Master takes time for themselves each day. Whether it is in the morning when the energies of earth are quiet and just awakening, or deep in the night when everything is still, the Master takes time to accept – not to critique or analyze but to *accept* – their creation. It is only when you have full acceptance that you can start to truly allow the changes. Full acceptance of who you are – every part of you – is required before you begin to understand how the changes within actually take place.

Next is the full acceptance of all things around you, the world around you, the people around you. However, it is very difficult to accept other people, politics, events of the world, its leaders, its religions, all of these things, when you're not accepting yourself. Once you start working with the acceptance of yourself in this Now moment, then you can look out into the world and begin accepting it for what it is. Yes, the world has its difficulties and its struggles but it is no more than children playing games with each other. Yes, there are things that you would like to be better or easier, but you have to understand that humans are choosing this. It is their creation, their game. Whether they pollute the earth, whether they have wars or famine, they are choosing all of this.

It is not until you come to the point of acceptance that you can really understand how these energies are being created in the first place. When you accept *what is* then you will understand the dynamics behind all of these things taking place. And, with that total compassion and acceptance, then you will have the wisdom to know what you could or should do – if anything. With that perspective of wisdom that you will have, you will shine out amongst the other humans as a beacon for those who *are* ready for change and transformation.

GOD

In the previous sections we talked about the New Energy Master's relationship with themselves. We talked about the relationship with others, all the dynamics that take place in dealing with other people, and events in the world. Now we're going to talk about the relationship with Spirit. Let's call it God.

This whole concept of grander beings – which is all gods are – was not really known or understood during the Lemurian periods of humanity and even through most of the Atlantean periods. There was no word to describe God, there were no religions, there was no worship as you know it now. Religions, you see, are a contemporary invention of mankind.

In Lemuria and Atlantis it was simply called the Unknown. It was acknowledged that we don't understand how certain things happen, but it wasn't attributed to some higher power. It was simply What Has Not Been Learned Yet. That's all it was. There wasn't some great deification taking place, there weren't temples, there wasn't worship and there weren't any rules. It was simply What Has Not Been Learned Yet. It was beautiful. It was the acceptance that there were things yet to be discovered as well as the acceptance that much had already been discovered.

It wasn't until approximately nine thousand years ago that the first true concept of gods came into being. Human consciousness had changed and developed enough that there was now a need to try to define this thing that had not yet been learned. So humans came up with this concept of gods. In a sense they were, at that time, moving in the right direction. For instance they understood that there was a god of the sun and, in a sense, there is. There is an energy of the sun, a consciousness of the sun, so humans at that time called it a god, because they didn't understand it or how it worked or interrelated to them and to nature. Because of this lack of understanding they feared it and therefore worshiped it.

They felt that there was a god of the waters. Because they didn't understand the waters but knew it was essential to life, they feared it and then they worshiped it. They created a god of the waters. They did the same with the air. They did the same with the earth itself. They could, at some level, perceive the energy of these things but they didn't understand it, they feared it, and then worshiped it.

They did the same thing with the animals. They had gods of the birds, and in a sense there is because there is a consciousness of birds, even of the individual species of birds. That is how birds interconnect with each other, no matter how you define it in scientific terms. They connect with their group bird consciousness and they are able to fly in a flock. They are able to have the same movements and patterns with each other without having to speak, or use a language because they are using a language of consciousness. So you could say there is a god or a consciousness of birds.

You can take any grouping on earth, whether it is of humans or animals or parts of nature, and it has it's own group consciousness. Until approximately ten thousand years ago these different consciousnesses were defined as "gods."

Then along comes Abraham who decides that there should be just one God. Actually this was an evolution again in consciousness, this understanding that things do have a oneness. It also had gotten very boring and very tedious to worship *all* of these different gods. Back in that era humans would have dozens, perhaps hundreds of statues in their homes to all of the different gods, representing all the different unknowns and all of the different fears that they had.

Abraham came up with the concept of *one God*. He made it simple, elegantly simple. He said "I don't want to have to buy all these statues, I'll just have one! I don't have enough time in the day to say prayers and worship all of these different gods, I'll just go to one." He was very efficient!

The idea caught on quickly because the other people were also tired of worshiping all these different gods and having all these different fears. Now it could be consolidated into one fear alone. This idea of one God caught on quickly and became the basis for the Jewish religion, the Christian religion and even the Islamic religions. These are the religions that are predominant in the world right now and they all believe in one God.

Throughout the last several thousand years this image of the one God has been defined and molded and shaped by humans – humans who still have fear and humans who also realize "This is a wonderful way to control and manipulate, a wonderful way to perpetuate this whole process of hypnosis." Humans created a God in heaven and they created also the antithesis of God – the Devil, Satan. Then they put fear, not just around Satan but around God as well, and created this tremendous duality. They have written books about it and then they've said "This book is holy" – even though there are many different versions of it. They say "This book cannot be changed" – although it has been changed innumerable times. They say "This is *the* sacred book and you must worship it" – even though they themselves don't necessarily worship it.

You have this whole institution, actually this whole business and consciousness, centered around this contemporary version of God. But God is still the Unknown. There are all these laws and rules about how to live in accordance with God's rules, but it is a God from some far-off and distant place. This whole concept of God, combined with the concept of death, puts a tremendous overlay of fear and limitation on humans all across the world.

The Master of the New Energy lets all of this go. The Master of the New Energy understands that the concept of God comes from the consciousness of humans all over the earth, but it doesn't have to be *their* concept.

I will make a bold statement here: As you go along this path of your enlightenment – especially if you come from some type of religious or even spiritual background – there comes a point in your self-discovery where it is best to just let go of God. Let go of the whole concept, the word, the idea – even of Spirit. It is best almost to become an atheist and let all of that go because the overlays in the concept of God are extremely heavy. They twist and distort and pervert the true understanding so it is best just to let them go. It is best to say your farewells to God.

Now obviously this is going to push some of the largest buttons ever because humans have been trained to fear this thing called God. Nearly all humans have their own personal versions of the grand God, the God they think or feel or believe that they are talking to, the God that they call upon in the dark and difficult times in their life, the God that they pray to.

Letting go of the concept of God also brings up the fear that when you release this you're going to allow God's antithesis, God's nemesis, to come in. There is this great fear that you're going to allow Satan into your life because that's what you've been told. "The minute you let go of God, Satan's going to move in and take over." So it potentially creates some very difficult, very nasty energies of fear when I say to let go of God.

The Master understands that the concept of God they once held was simply an evolution in their understanding. The Master also truly understands that they didn't have a perfect relationship with God. So often they felt abandoned, and left out by God. They felt that God didn't truly hear them, that they had to ring little bells in order to summon God. The relationship was distant at best, dysfunctional most likely. There comes a point on the path, as the Master is reviewing their evolution, that it is time to leave God at the side of the road.

This is a difficult, challenging thing. It brings up issues in this lifetime and in many other lifetimes, issues that are deep, issues that are woven into the fabric of the deep inner consciousness. But there comes a point where it is necessary to develop a new relationship with God.

Let's not even use the word "God" at this point. That is an old word, weighed down with Old Energy. In some of the ancient writings the word "God" wasn't even written. There were words that conveyed the meaning such as YHWH, Jehovah. Sometimes it was portrayed as the Four Letters That Cannot Be Spoken. Most of the time this thing you now call Spirit, formerly God, was simply not uttered. It was understood what you meant to say but it was not uttered.

It wasn't for being so reverent that you couldn't say YHWH, the word "God." It was a respect and understanding by the Masters back then that this concept of God was simply unspeakable. They understood that the moment you would speak the concept in human language you would lose its energy, its indescribable, beautiful energy. So for quite a while the word "God" wasn't even spoken, it was just felt.

The relationship with what I will just call the Unknown can be known. It is a very personal relationship because *it is the relationship with yourself*. It is how you relate to You. You are used to relating to yourself on a very human and limited level and relating to God on some far-off, distant and mighty level. You tend to think of God as all-knowing, all-present, but *you* have created that separation, that chasm.

Now, as a Master in the New Energy, you develop a whole new relationship with What Has Yet To Be Learned, What Has Yet To Be Felt, What Has Yet To Be Understood.

You could say that it will always be Yet To Be Understood because even as you develop this relationship with the Unspoken of yourself, the Unknown of yourself, there is always more to know and discover. It is endless and it occurs right here within you. It doesn't come from any church. It doesn't come from a temple built of stone and wood. It doesn't come from any of the angelic beings, for many of them still have yet to experience What Has Yet To Be Learned.

This is very difficult to put into words or describe in human terms, but it is a new relationship with What Has Yet To Be Learned. It is you, but it is much more than you. It is within, but it encompasses so much more as well. You are a partner and a participant, and yet it is all of you.

You see? We run into this point of just not being able to define it anymore. That is why we say the New Energy Master sets down their old beliefs and old concepts of God, says farewell to Spirit – because that was just a concept – and invites within themselves What Has Yet To Be Discovered.

Take a look at your relationship with your former God. Did you believe that God knows everything? Perhaps God doesn't. Did you believe that God is everywhere? Perhaps God isn't. Did you believe that God can heal and mend all things? Perhaps He or She cannot.

Take a look at every thought, every feeling and every prayer that you have ever prayed; take a look at your relationship with God. The Master understands it is time to put that down and let it go so that they can develop the *new* relationship with What Has Yet To Be Discovered.

I won't say anything more about this because words now would just go in circles. They would spin, they would cause you to go intellectual. Now, it is just a blank. Now, it is time to simply let go so that you can move forward in the new way.

THE MAGIC OF MASTERY

The magic begins occurring for the Master at this point. They have let go of some of the deepest and most limiting beliefs they have held about themselves, which also happen to be the beliefs and the limitations they had about God. Now the Master is free and clear.

The Master understands there is nothing, but in that nothing there can be anything. In other words, there is not a predetermined path or a karmic course that they must follow. It is all right here in this Now and, essentially, there is nothing until the Master starts choosing. The magic comes in now because the limitations from the past are gone.

What is magic? Magic is simply what cannot be defined yet. Everything is magic when you take a look at it. Everything is beautiful and phenomenal in the way it works. It is only when the human mind comes to understand it in definable, analytical terms that there is no longer any magic to it.

Magic means a certain excitement, a certain discovery taking place. Magic means tapping into the unknown, bringing it into this reality and allowing it to unfold and operate. The magic goes out of magic only when you understand how it actually works, when you can dissect it and put it into human or mathematical terms, when you can put a structure around it – or at least you think you can.

Merlin

Let's talk about Merlin. Many of you relate Merlin to the energy of this character from the time of King Arthur and Camelot, but Merlin was not a single person. Merlin actually has it's beginnings approximately five to six hundred B.C.E., Before Current Era. The essence or the origin of Merlin actually begins in the places that you now know as Hungary and Romania. It was there that small groups of humans stepped out of society, fled their countries and their communities, because they knew that there was more. They were tired of being dictated what to believe and how to believe it so they set out to create a consciousness of magic, of going beyond.

The word Merlin itself simply means "One who goes beyond." "The expanded one." Other interpretations are "One who sees beyond" or "The Seer of things."

This group of humans, starting what we would consider to be one of the first contemporary mystery schools, allowed themselves to go beyond. They were true explorers in consciousness. They let go of the fears of demons and dragons and gods and created their own type of safe and sacred space where they could expand their energies. They helped to create this entity that you now know as Merlin the Magician.

They chose to have Merlin represented or embodied by one individual at a time, so there have been many Merlins, one after the other, for approximately the past twenty-five hundred years. This Merlin energy became more prevalent and more noticeable, particularly about five hundred years after the death of Yeshua. It became a regular part of society, it didn't have to be in strict hiding anymore, no longer having to hide in the caves and deep forests. It could come out.

The Merlin energy, particularly the one you know from the legends of King Arthur, had to do with the hope of humanity, the magic and the undiscovered potentials of humanity. As you know, Merlin represented the magic, and represented the energy of the Druids as well. Merlin was particularly noticeable around the time when the new Christian energy was coming into the lands. Even though the energies of Merlin and Arthur worked together, they also opposed each other. That is an interesting story of duality in itself. One energy, represented by Arthur, was it's the way *into* consciousness; the other energy, represented by Merlin, was on it's way back out.

As we come into the new era now, Merlin doesn't have to be represented by a single individual or even a small group of individuals.

Now the New Energy Masters understand that *they* are the Merlins. They are the ones who go beyond, the ones who understand that all of this is a very real illusion. They understand that energy truly does not have structure. It can *be* structured temporarily to serve the needs of its creator but it contains no essential structure of its own.

The Masters of New Energy, the new Merlins, understand that just because something is not recognized or understood by science does not mean it is not real. Look at history over the past few thousand years. There are things that are being done now that would be considered magic just a hundred years ago. Things are taken for granted now that would be considered evil or at least spiritually suspicious not even five hundred years ago. They would be feared.

The Master of the New Energy understands that *anything* can be done. You *can* go beyond. You are not limited to your physical body or your physical environment, but yet you can be fully present within it. You are not limited to the old laws of physics because those laws are changing as consciousness is changing. There are those who would tell you that the laws of physics are unchangeable, that this is just the way it is. But the new Merlin understands that this is only *one* way that it is. There are many other ways as well.

The Merlin understands that they can shape and shift energy in any way that they choose – as long as they are willing to go beyond. The new Merlin must be willing to go beyond what is currently known by man and by science, and beyond what is currently accepted by religion and even by philosophy.

The Merlin understands that they will always return to their core and this is a very essential and important part of the wisdom of the Master. Many of you have feared going beyond, expanding yourself multi-dimensionally, because you were afraid you would lose your basis, your foundation. Up until now you were probably right. You probably would have lost contact with your human identity in this reality. Your human identity sits at one point in time and space – and, we would also add, experience – and if you expanded too far, if you went beyond in the way that the Merlins of the past did, there was a very good chance that you would lose this point with yourself and become disassociated.

The humans who have what you would call a more primitive or slower level of consciousness, and who attempt to do this journey far beyond, do have the tendency to have things happen to them such as fragmenting their personalities. They tend to get into things like multiple personality disorder where fragments of them sit in other realms and other dimensions, literally existing on those levels. Then they not only have their life and their aspect here on earth but now they are living in multiple realms. It is very difficult and very, very confusing on the living entity, the human self.

But the Master, having come into full acceptance of themselves and the reality that surrounds them, having let go of the old concepts of God – which was basically fear – is now free to explore the Unknown or the Yet To Be Known. You see, there is a direct correlation between the Yet To Be Known and the concept of Spirit.

The important point here is that the Merlin, the New Energy Master, can now explore and expand into these other realms fairly effortlessly, with ease and grace, knowing they will always return to themselves. The New Energy Master knows that they will no longer get lost in the array of dimensions or lose themselves in all the activities that are going on outside of their physical or known reality. The Merlin always finds their way back home because they create a home space within them, here in this Now reality, that is so inviting and so safe that all of them always comes back.

You see, when you are not accepting yourself; when you are hating your body; when you are fighting your mind; when you are not accepting the world around you; it is very difficult to go out into these multi-dimensional expansions where you can shape and shift energy any way you envision it – and then fully come back home. Until now, home has *not* been a friendly place. This reality, your body, this time and space and experience, has not felt welcoming for your energy to come back home to. It has felt chaotic, confusing and uninviting. But now, in the mastery of the New Energy, you can create a space that *is* yours, that *is* welcoming and inviting, that *is* home. It *is* you and it is *within* you.

Now you are free to go out and explore, free to play with energies in a way that you never have before. You can let your mind go and be free in a way that you haven't been in a long time. You have trapped your mind, isolated it, protected it, locked the door and closed the windows. You have limited it because of the fear of what would happen if you opened up and expanded. You've done the same with your own spirit, keeping it in hiding somewhere to protect it, to keep it away from what you considered to be this harsh reality.

But now you are free to expand. You are free to let yourself go crazy, to expand your etheric energy, not just in this dimension but in all dimensions. And you are free, more than anything, not to have to understand what you are experiencing. This is another very important concept.

Your limitations have been caused by the mind's inability to comprehend what was going on. You have been trained to be a mental being so any time you felt your energy venturing beyond, venturing into places and consciousnesses that the mind could no longer comprehend, everything came to a stop. You prevented yourself from traveling and playing in these other realms, and energy fields because you couldn't take your mind with you.

But now you are free to open up, free to go beyond, and not need to have the mind understand everything. There comes a point where the mind simply *cannot* comprehend. It is not designed for that, it's not tuned or trained for that because it was designed to function in the human reality and the earth energies. Now you can go beyond and not have to think it in your mind.

This was the beauty and the elegance of the original creation of the Merlin energy – the freedom not to have to know it in the mind – and it is a very important part of creating this Merlin energy in your life. Again, words are difficult here because how do you explain something that cannot be put into words? How do you define something that cannot be defined? It just is.

The Master understands that it can be experienced even though it doesn't have to be understood. The Master understands that you can experience something and not analyze it, not structure it or define it. This is the essence of the Merlin, the essence of the magic.

Now, having fully accepted themselves and the world, having let go of the old barriers and limitations, the Master now allows themselves to *experience* at all levels. You give yourself the freedom to play with energies. You give yourself the freedom to expand in every different way *without limitations*. The Master understands there is no right or wrong, there are no rules anymore.

This is one thing the Merlin deeply understands: No rules, for they limit the self. There are no rules out here, in these mass multiple dimensions. *There are no rules.* There are no rules about gravity, no rules about force, no rules about duality or any of those other things. It is all free and clear and now you, as a Master in the New Energy, can go play.

These concepts are very simple. There may be a tendency to try to over-think them, to try to create the rules around them, but in the end the Master understands there truly are no rules.

There is Self.

There is Experience.

And there is Expression.

Let us take a deep breath together.

As you have been reading these words a tremendous amount of consciousness has come through you. Some of it your eyes have seen, much of it has been conveyed to you at many different levels. So as we come to the end of this portion of the Master's Guide to the New Energy, let yourself play with what has been discussed. Let yourself experience the new Unknown.

TRUSTING, KNOWING AND MASTERY

I began this book with a discussion about trust in Self. It is the single biggest ingredient in becoming a Master and it is the ingredient of moving into the New Energy. If you don't trust yourself you are leaving parts of you behind. If you don't trust yourself you are taking a very crooked and distorted path into the New Energy. You'll get there sooner or later, but it's going to be the tough and difficult path.

Having undeniable, implicit and total trust in yourself – and total compassion with yourself – is the key. It is the secret to Mastery. You don't need to write volumes about it, you don't have to have long schools and classes about it – it just is. You just choose it. It is elegantly simple and yet some make it so difficult and complex.

As you trust yourself more and more each day you open to who you really are, not just the identity that you have right now but to the *true* You. As you open to yourself through trust you're going to discover what the Unknown, what the Unexplainable truly is and you'll understand why it is difficult to put a word on it. You will understand why we don't even like using words such as "Spirit" or "God" to define it any more, and you will discover that it is already within – but not trapped within or limited to within. It is within you but it is a part of you that is so expansive it is indescribable. It cannot be defined, only discovered and experienced.

I also talked about the Merlin energy. The Merlin is the one who goes into the unknown. The discoverer, the explorer. I talked about this whole concept of magic, which is nothing more than what you have yet to know or understand.

Let's combine the two here for a moment in a brief exercise. I'm going to quickly ask you a series of questions and you're going to *trust* yourself and the answer that comes to you. It *will* come from you. It's not coming from any outside energy, the answer is coming only from you. Ask yourself these questions out loud, then wait no more than two seconds to feel the immediate answer:

What is the title of your first book? *[handwritten]*

What is the name of the first song you're going to write? *[handwritten]*

How are you going to bring financial abundance into your life? *[handwritten]*

What is the most important thing you can do in your relationships with other people right now? *[handwritten]*

You see, we're going fast and you're trying to say "Slow down, I need time for the answer," but that's because you're trying to *think* about the answer. Here is where the Merlin energy comes in, the trust comes in where you're just *feeling* it. You're not going to hear words here, you're just going to feel *something*, even though it may be undefinable. It may just be a knowingness or a feeling.

Here are more questions:

What is the best thing you can do for your body right now? *[handwritten]*

What is the name that most fits you in this present moment? *[handwritten]*

What do your correspondent angels look like? *[handwritten]*

What is your favorite game to play? *[handwritten]*

What was the most important thing about your early childhood years? *[handwritten]*

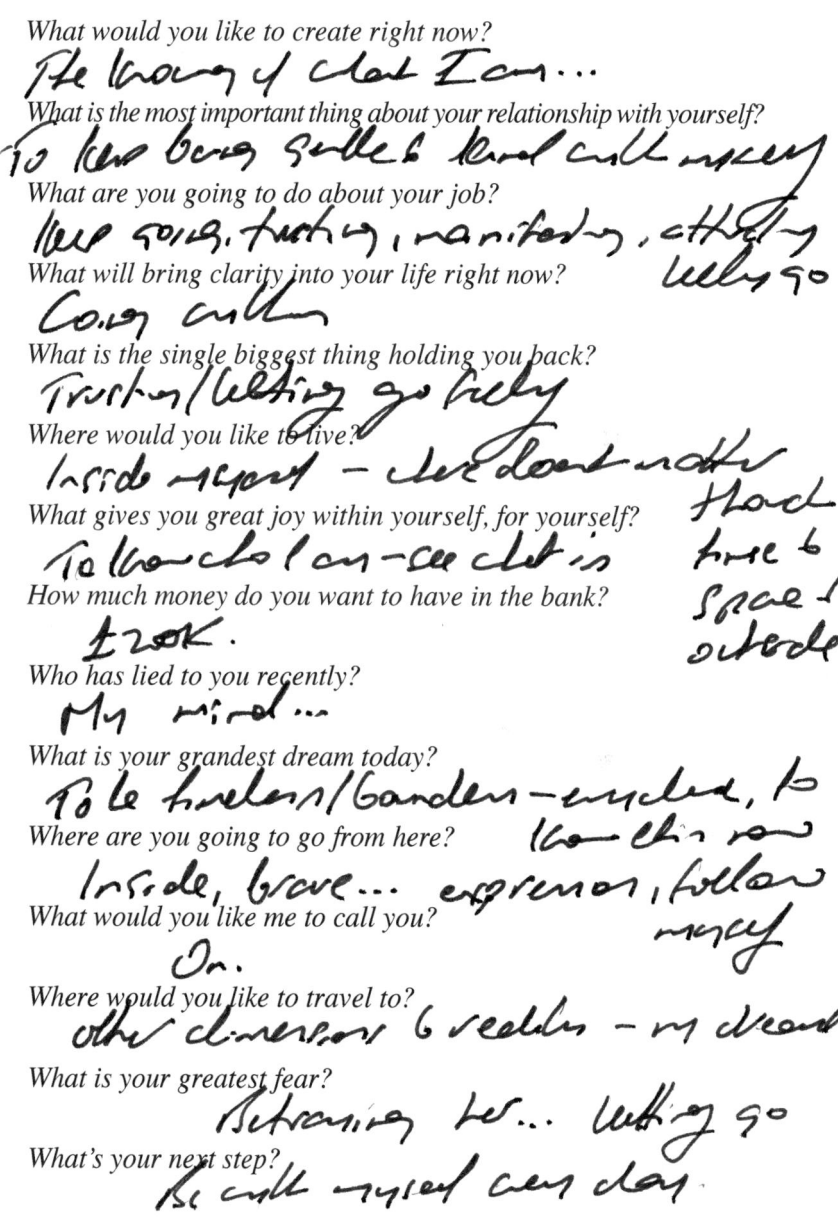

What would you like to create right now?
The knowing of what I am...

What is the most important thing about your relationship with yourself?
To keep being gentle & kind with myself

What are you going to do about your job?
Keep going, trusting, manifesting, others... letting go

What will bring clarity into your life right now?
Going within

What is the single biggest thing holding you back?
Trusting / letting go fully

Where would you like to live?
Inside myself — doesn't matter
Had time to space & outside

What gives you great joy within yourself, for yourself?
To know who I am — see what is

How much money do you want to have in the bank?
£20K.

Who has lied to you recently?
My mind...

What is your grandest dream today?
To be timeless / boundless — encircled, to

Where are you going to go from here?
Inside, brave... expression, follow

What would you like me to call you?
On.
myself

Where would you like to travel to?
other dimensions & realms — my dream

What is your greatest fear?
Betraying self... letting go

What's your next step?
Be with myself each day.

You see, there *is* an answer. It was there because the answers to any of these questions are in your field of consciousness or potential. Perhaps you haven't recognized the answer, perhaps you've been avoiding the answer. Part of you was even denying it as the answers came. But every answer that you came up with – *trust it*.

You say "But I didn't have time to think about it, it just came. It was crazy!" It's not crazy, there's a reason it came to you. Now, the answer – and the reason for the answer – may have many layers or levels and you may have been perceiving only one. As you explore the answers that you just gave yourself, explore the other facets of each answer as well. As I said before it is always about going into more depth with the energy, going into the other layers. But do it without thinking. Do it in the same consciousness that you just answered these questions.

There is a tendency to trivialize what you heard and say "I don't know where that came from." It came from you, from your own energy field. It has been sitting there waiting for the opportunity to fly in and address itself and it knew it had to jump in quick while the opportunity was present.

Remember this. It *is* this simple. This is a little game you can play any time. Ask any questions. Have somebody ask them to you. Do it with your group of Shaumbra – but then *trust the answers*, no matter how difficult they seem to be. Perhaps it was a negative answer, perhaps it wasn't what you wanted to hear, but there was a reason it came to you.

You see, this is what the Merlins have always known. They didn't get bogged down with the intellectual analysis because if they did, well, they wouldn't have been Merlins. They would have gotten stuck and they would have never been able to traverse the dimensions, never been able to change their reality landscapes.

As simple as this exercise was, remember its energy because that's what it's like being the Merlin, being the Master. It is the intuitive knowingness and the acceptance of what comes through. It is that implicit trust of just letting the answer come in.

Now, perhaps you say "I received no answer." Yes you did. You were looking for something specific, searching for words, for instance, and the answer might have come in with just a feeling. The answer might have come in with a quick picture or a flash of knowingness. The answer might have been only one word, or you may have heard a whole sentence or paragraph being spoken and you were trying to decipher it. But the essence is still there and will remain there. You can go back to any of the questions at any time and ask yourself what you were feeling in that moment.

Take a deep breath and remember how simple that was, and remember it is the experience of trusting *yourself*. It didn't come from anywhere else. There are many angelic beings with you, overseeing this exercise to make sure that no other energies interfere. It wasn't anybody else, the answers came from you.

QUESTIONS AND ANSWERS

QUESTION 1: There's a part of me that really knows I am magnificent, that I am a Master and a true creator. Yet another part of me feels great hurt and sadness, feels tired and disillusioned. How can I accept that part without overruling it and without letting it overrule the Master part? I feel this has something to do with balancing my masculine and feminine energies. Can you comment on this?

SAINT-GERMAIN: Indeed. First of all, you're getting a bit caught up here in a bit of intellectualizing. I understand your heart is very much into this question but you've gone intellectual on yourself. You're trying to dissect and analyze this whole thing and you can let that go now.

Realize that, even as a Master, you *do* have parts of yourself that feel insecure, that feel little, because that's an experience that you've given yourself. You've created it. Don't try to deny that part of yourself but don't let it rule over your kingdom, over your domain. Rise above it. Understand it is just an aspect, it's just a part of you, and then *choose*. Energize yourself towards the Master that you want to be. Then this energy of what you might call the puny human, the puny or limited "master," will soon see that it was a master, it was creating it's reality – but it was stuck. Very soon it will get back into a type of a synchronized dance with the rest of you.

With this whole thing of mastery the one caution I would give is that is can get intellectual very easily because you start trying to force yourself to believe that you're a Master but yet you don't really feel it. That is why I say to examine all of the facets of yourself. Stand back, look at how you have been creating all of this and then, when you feel ready, breathe in and *accept* the fact that you are a Master and a creator.

It ultimately comes back to the point of trusting yourself, for that is the fundamental principle of the Master of the New Energy. One hundred percent implicit, undeniable trust in yourself. It is a paradox because it is a surrender to yourself – not to an outside entity but to yourself – and at the same time a total acceptance of yourself. You are surrendering the facade, the illusion of the identity, and accepting the fullness of who you are. You're reaching the level of full and total trust and that is what this is all about.

I'm going to ask you to continue feeling this rather than just thinking about it. You can get caught up in thinking but I'm asking you to *feel* your grandness. Feel what it is like, with each breath, as you trust yourself. Ah, this brings up all sorts of issues, all sorts of questions. You will encounter a lot of blocks along the way but in each moment, with each breath, sink into your own deep trust of yourself.

QUESTION 2: Would you comment about being a Master when it comes to relationships around you? I'm not speaking of clients or students but rather things like teenagers, in-laws, ex-spouses. When there are a lot of drama energies around you, please speak of Mastership in that situation.

SAINT-GERMAIN: Indeed. Probably the most difficult and challenging; how to be a Master when surrounded by other humans – particularly those who challenge you in so many different ways!

As you make your choice on how you want to arrive at your Mastership, and as you sink deep into trusting yourself, those around you who are energetically connected with you are going to feel something shifting. Many of them are going to rebel and object because they are used to feeding off of you. They are used to the way your energy operated and now they feel something has just shifted. They are going to act out, perhaps become more dramatic than ever before, and they might do some interesting things.

Let's say, for instance, you are energetically disconnecting from your family. You know it's important to serve yourself first so there's a period of disconnecting. It's not that you don't love them or care about them, it's not that you're selfish. It's that you know it is important to balance yourself right now. So what happens?

They feel that disconnection at some level and they do extreme things. Perhaps unconsciously but interconnectedly they do things like get hurt because they need the mother's attention and love. They need to be able to feed off the mother so they do something very dramatic like break a leg, get a large cut, or be in a car accident. These type of things can start happening unfortunately, but whose energy it is? Is it you or is it them? Are you making it happen or are they creating it? And now the question is, are you going to get sucked into the drama? Are you going to stop serving yourself first in order to continue playing in their drama, participating in their stage play?

It's very difficult, I know, because, particularly with parents and lovers it tears at the deepest issues inside of you. You're going to feel selfish, you're going to feel that you're abandoning those around you. But are those really your feelings or are they being projected onto you by others?

You're asking my advice. I'm going to make a very bold statement here: *Disconnect*. Disconnect from your families – those are karmic zoos in my opinion! Disconnect from your spouses, from your soul mates, from your children, all of these things. Disconnect even from Shaumbra.

Now, this begs the definition of disconnecting, and it also brings of issues of abandonment and lots of other things. Stop. Take a deep breath. Trust yourself. You're not running from anybody, you're not walking out on anybody. You are actually becoming self-integrated and self-sufficient and you're just not allowing them to feed off of you any more – and you don't need to feed off of them either.

It doesn't mean you have to pack your bags and leave the house. Perhaps you may have to but it doesn't *mean* you have to. It doesn't mean that you have to sever the relationship. It just means disconnecting from the Old Energy tentacles that you had with other people so that you can be the sovereign Master that you are. As I said in an earlier segment, you are self-contained. You don't need to feed on anybody.

A very good question and a difficult question and I do not mean to trivialize it in any way. But sooner or later you're going to have to disconnect from all the ones around you.

What is the purest relationship of all? The relationship with yourself, first. What is the purest relationship with another Being, whether it is human or angelic? When they are two complete selves and don't need each other to complete themselves. Trying to complete yourself through another Being never works and sooner or later it will break up. But when there are two Beings who are sovereign, the love that can be shared and expressed – and the joy that can be experienced – is far beyond the old way of relationships. Thank you.

QUESTION 3: I have been confronted with being very close to death and now I am trying to start living again. I feel life is coming towards me from all sides, the circumstances around me are very positive and supporting. Yet somewhere I feel I do not let all these in. Why? I really feel it very strongly that I do not let it in.

SAINT-GERMAIN: Yes. What is the first thing that we spoke of today?

QUESTIONER 3: First thing? Trust.

SAINT-GERMAIN: Yes, trust indeed. There is sometimes a reluctance to let these life energies come in, whether they are in a form of just pure energy or other humans or anything, because humans fall out of trust with themselves.

You have had, by the way, a number of near-death type of encounters in your life, not just one. You've been riding right on the edge – on many occasions, sorry to say – so you've developed a type of spiritual callous, a hard spiritual layer around you. It is from a lack of trusting yourself and a lack of trusting others. There are several occasions in this lifetime when you were counting on others to keep you from these dangerous situations and they did not. So you closed up – not just to trusting them but yourself as well – and shut down many aspects of yourself.

So now, as you are choosing life and feeling the energies trying to come in, you still have this wall around you. It's time to let that down, time to let it dissolve and go away. These energies that want to come in are here to serve you. Any energies that would harm you cannot come in, not because you are so strong or you have these defenses or barriers but because you're choosing life, because you're choosing to *be* a Master.

So I'm going to ask you, through the breathing and even through taking baths, to start letting down these walls and coming back into trust with yourself. You are wise and magnificent, you are a Master. Now trust yourself that the highest order of things are going to come into your life.

QUESTION 4: Sometimes I find myself struggling between trusting myself and taking action by making a choice. I've used trust as an excuse not to make a choice until I have to. Can you shed some light on this issue or make some suggestions to make this easier?

SAINT-GERMAIN: I think you've already answered your own question! That is indeed one of the biggest challenges because humans are afraid to make choices until they trust the situation. And that generally leads to an intellectual analysis of the situation, which leads to a blockage of trust, which leads to not making a choice. You see how all of this works so beautifully together?

Do you know what trust is? Trust is just jumping into that pool without worrying about how cold the water is or how deep the water is or what monsters lie beneath. That is what trust is. But the good news is that it's your own pool. Any monsters in there are yours, if somebody's peed in the pool it's only you, and the temperature is the temperature of your own heart.

What do you have to lose, Shaumbra? Jump into your own pool. Trust yourself. Then be bold and daring and courageous and *make some choices*. Just start choosing – but not from the human desperation level. Make grand choices. "I choose to be a grand painter." "I choose to write books." "I choose to be happy." "I choose to travel around the world." What I'm saying is that the choices should be from a place of joy and creation, not from need and desperation.

Start making choices and then *get out of your way*. You've just energized yourself to start bringing in the energies to make it happen, you've adjusted yourself so that now the appropriate energies can come in. But as they do, understand it's probably going to be grander than what you originally chose or thought you would create, and it's also probably going to be different than what you expected. We said in an earlier segment, "Don't limit the outcome." Let go of the expectations so that the choices, the creations – and your Mastery – can be grand.

QUESTION 5: I've got a question from the readers of this book. I've read all of your books, I've read this one, sometimes it was breathtaking and there's great ideas, but where do I start? What's in the user guide to this book? I know that the people who are leading the workshops or the courses I follow can become Masters, there are big Masters in other dimensions, but surely it's not *me* who's going to become a Master. So where do I start?

SAINT-GERMAIN: Excellent. Where *do* you start? Anywhere you want! But you see, the important thing is to *start*. I don't want to over-define when and how to start, it will occur as a natural potential or opportunity within each individual human in their life. Something might come up, for instance, the very next day because, once the question is asked, "Where should I start," the opportunity appears. So understand, first of all, that the opportunity is going to be there and it will give you a jumping-in point or a launching point. It doesn't really matter where or what it is, it's a matter of now making a choice to begin the process.

You could say it *did* already start if you have chosen to be a Master. If you're just choosing to think about being a Master, contemplate being a Master, then that will be the total sphere of your choices and potentials. But if you've truly said "I am ready to be the Master," then it doesn't matter where the process starts. It will unfold naturally, simply and elegantly for each in their own way.

That is where the wise Teacher Master comes in also but there is no formula in this. I'm giving you guidelines and discussion points in this book. It doesn't matter if you start on page 1 or page 100. It only matters that you are jumping into the energy and then allowing it to unfold.

As you teach this, as all of Shaumbra are given the opportunity to teach from this book, make sure not to set up too many methods or procedures or processes. It is individual with each student, case by case by case. Let them start anywhere.

QUESTION 6: What exercises, for example, can you do with clients to help them discover the different layers?

SAINT-GERMAIN: What can you do with your clients – with yourself, even – to understand or perceive all the layers? The first thing is to know that there are many layers. When you look at that rock and say "It's just a rock," well, you are only looking at or perceiving one layer.

Let's use the rock as an example. A good place to start is to have them look at the rock and define it. Then have them smell the rock. You say "Well rocks don't smell, they're rocks!" Ah, rocks *do* have a smell and that smell – some of you even call this aromatherapy – can start triggering other layers and levels. Have them touch the rock. Have them listen to the rock. It may sound crazy but rocks talk. They don't talk English or German or Dutch but they speak, they transmit energy.

Once you've gotten your clients or yourself discovering the other layers at the human sensory level, now have them feel into the other levels. You're crossing a big chasm here because you're asking them to go from definable to somewhat undefinable. But have them feel what else is in that rock. Encourage them to open their imagination.

One of the things that I've done in my mystery schools in the past was teach them to literally have part of their energy start circling around the rock or object; and then go into it; and then imagine themselves going into the other dimensions around it. It is an imagination exercise. Some of your students are going to doubt themselves and say "Well, this is crazy, but in this rock I see a face of a man." Obviously there is not a face of a man in the rock, but perhaps they are perceiving a man who touched that rock a hundred years ago. Have them open the imagination, realize that there are many layers and level, and understand that *there are no wrong answers*.

Through this type of exploration they're going to discover that every object – everything – has many layers and levels to it and it is wonderfully fun to start playing in the layers. The carpet beneath you right now, it's not just a poorly designed carpet! It contains the energy of thousands and thousands of people who have sat in this room before. Their energy is now part of the composition, the energetic fabric of the carpet.

Allow yourself to feel the group that was in here a week ago, or several weeks ago. A year ago. You see, their energy is here as well. Perhaps you're feeling a very boring business meeting. Perhaps you're feeling some type of sales motivational meeting and its phoniness, its pretend type of nature. It's all in there.

And the interesting thing is, as long as you trust yourself there are really no wrong answers, because you might not only be tapping into the energy of that carpet and the group that was in here a week ago, but now you can use that energy to travel multi-dimensionally somewhere else. You see, you can pick any point, any tangible object and use that to essentially travel through time and space.

QUESTION 7: I have strong physical reactions in my current relationship situation. I also have difficulties in expressing love and receiving it. I would like to have more clarity in this situation. Thank you.

SAINT-GERMAIN: Indeed. At a very simple, basic level the issues that you are having with the love relationships is really about the love in your own life with yourself. You have blocked off the love within yourself. As you go back to the complete trust in self you can't help but love yourself. When you allow yourself to trust, you discover new parts – or even old parts – of yourself that have been blocked and you just can't help but love and accept yourself. As you get to this point of truly loving yourself don't be afraid to hug yourself. Don't be afraid to admire yourself. Don't be afraid to honor yourself for what you do. Love yourself in every way.

You have been in a long pattern of self abuse and self neglect and at this point it is vital that you love yourself. The relationships are secondary, they tend to work themselves out when you love yourself first. It is only when you don't love yourself that you see this reflected in outside relationships. So, to try to correct the outside relationship without loving your inside relationship is basically futile. It will be very temporary.

QUESTION 8: Any suggestions for how to teach mastery to young kids, say 4-12 years old?

SAINT-GERMAIN: This book has been designed so that even the young ones will be able to understand it. There may need to be some age-appropriate interpretations by those who will teach this but the material is the same for the young as it is for the not so young.

QUESTION 9: I have felt, for the last one and a half years, a huge pressure in my throat. It is even physically hurting and pushing my tongue up and I wonder if you could help me understand it?

SAINT-GERMAIN: I'm going to ask you, what is causing this pressure?

QUESTIONER 9: I hoped *you* could tell me that because I'm not sure. I think it has to do with stepping into my power.

SAINT-GERMAIN: And stepping into your power in what way? Through what activities?

QUESTIONER 9: I think it has to do with communication but I cannot really give it a place inside of me. I don't know.

SAINT-GERMAIN: Yes, you *do* know. You're only pretending that you don't know because you're answering your own questions almost exactly as I would answer them. It is about communication. First of all, it is about stepping into your own voice, not using the voice of others. In other words speaking your ideas, sharing what you know rather than repeating what you have heard from somebody else. It is about saying it with your essence and letting it come through. It is right there within you, right now. You're just not letting it come up.

As you allow it to come through you can do things like speaking in front of groups or singing. You can also do one-on-one discussions with others, but this is truly not a very complex matter. It is simply about allowing your own voice to come through. The energy has been blocked and it wants to come through. Being blocked right there simply means that you have tremendous capability through the voice and through the communication. So let it come through. Don't think so much about it, just do it. Say, "Yes."

QUESTION 10: I would like to know more about integrating masculine and feminine energies. What can we do for this and can you give some more directions? Thank you.

SAINT-GERMAIN: You ask a very excellent question about the integration of your own masculine and feminine. These are two energies that have been separated for as long as energy itself has been separated into duality. When energy split into the elements of light and dark, negative and positive, at the same time it was also divided into the masculine/feminine and this has been part of the composition of the identities of those on the angelic side of the veil as well as those on the human side. When you come into human form you generally take on a very expressed, very pronounced form as either masculine or feminine.

It is time that these energies come back together and this is closely related to the love and acceptance of self. You no longer need to carry the wound of Isis, which is the feeling of failure, the feeling that you let someone down; and you no longer have to carry the energy of Adam, the feeling that you have to defend and protect. In the New Energy these come back together.

Breathing is a very important part. Simply understanding that you are both masculine and feminine is a very important part. And understanding that these two energies want to reunite with each other is important. You don't have to force them, for they *choose* to reunite now. It is about simply allowing this process.

QUESTION 11: My question is about abundance. It feels contradictory, what you said about having a servant in the real way of somebody looking after you, and still being self-dependent. So it's a big contradiction and I wonder if I'm going back to old habits of not having to take care of myself and finding somebody else who does it for me?

SAINT-GERMAIN: You need be more specific. Exactly what are you asking in this question? We understand you feel the contradiction but what would you like to know? Is it about abundance? Is it about service?

QUESTIONER 11: I'm creating abundance through somebody else. Well, somebody else provides me with a lot of money, so I don't have to...

SAINT-GERMAIN: I'm going to ask you to stop there. *You* are creating the abundance. Directly or indirectly – it matters not. If you are with somebody else who has abundance, you have helped to create this situation for yourself so that you are abundant also. Part of the denial here is that you are saying that you are not abundant, that someone else is. You are very abundant if you choose it. You are giving the power away to someone else when you say you have not created this wonderful set-up.

QUESTIONER 11: Are you saying I'm giving away my power?

SAINT-GERMAIN: I'm going to be very simple so everybody understands. Is there abundance in your life?

QUESTIONER 11: Yes.

SAINT-GERMAIN: End of discussion! You have created it. You are looking so hard, you're trying to over-analyze it. Do you have abundance in your life?

QUESTIONER 11: Yeah.

SAINT-GERMAIN: You have created it ... or did I create it for you?

QUESTIONER 11: No, I suppose I did.

SAINT-GERMAIN: I suppose! So this is what we mean about things being elegantly simple. You are trying to get too complex about it. *You have created it.* Now, if you find that it's a problem and there are strings attached – emotional or other types of manipulations taking place – that becomes another thing.

QUESTIONER 11: There are not anymore. There were in the beginning but I think that's done.

SAINT-GERMAIN: You're a brilliant creator. I admire you!

QUESTION 12: Can you please tell us something about the business my husband and I started. Why doesn't it seem to work?

SAINT-GERMAIN: There are numerous factors here. Both of you have quite a bit of fear, quite a bit of anxiety with this whole business. There is a lot on the line. You are putting much of yourself into this business in many different ways so there is a fear of its failure and this fear of failure itself actually helps to bring in that potential of failure, or at least limit the success.

You are brilliant creators, though sometimes you are creating things that you really don't want. You're creating more on what you might call the negative side rather than the positive. So take a look and address your fears, because so much is on the line. Not just your finances and your hard work but also your reputation, your good name, these type of things. Take a look at that fear and ask yourself if you choose it. Ask if it really belongs to you, ask if you want it to belong to you. If not, let it go.

Again we go back to the premise of this whole concept of being Masters: *It is time to trust yourself.* Trust what you are doing and let go of the expectation of the outcome. Oftentimes, especially in things like starting a business, there is expectation that you are going to have certain level of sales or customers. If you release that and simply allow the experiences to come, you're going to find so many more gifts in what you are doing. Even though it might not look like success, many other things are happening and becoming part of the process.

I will encourage you to definitely breathe through this process. Starting a business, being a creator, will always challenge core issues and, particularly here, we see the biggest issue is the fear of failure itself.

QUESTION 13: Earlier you talked about force versus flow. My question is regarding inner force. On the one hand I'm feeling a very strong inner force to step into my passion, whatever that may be. On the other hand I also feel the flow that says "Okay, it's going to come when it's going to come." So there's a bit of inner wrestling going on and I would like some more clarification on that.

SAINT-GERMAIN: There is a difference between force and desire. Desire has life to it, it has a passion, it has a feeling of expansion to it. Force, on the other hand, is a demanding energy. Demanding certain things, demanding a certain outcome, demanding that it has to happen in a certain way, pushing and forcing to make things happen.

So I'm saying to discern the difference between your passion and desire, your choices now coming into expression, versus forcing it, trying to make it happen. If you find that in trying to manifest this you're having to push everything, that everything is hard work, then take a second look – both at how you're letting the energy flow into your passion and desires, and how true you're being to your passion and desire. We know this is a small nuance but do you understand the difference?

QUESTIONER 13: Yes I do. I know it's not force, it's desire and I can feel that it's really there. On the other hand it's like something telling me "Okay, just wait, it's going to come." It's still like an inner wrestling and how do you deal with that?

SAINT-GERMAIN: That is a very difficult thing and that is what this mastery is all about. It is feeling the desire and the passion come up and, though it is strong, it is not necessarily the type of battling force I was talking about. So the strong passion and desire come up, and then it is about making the choice: Do you want to pursue this?

It will remain somewhat outside of you or elusive until you make that conscious choice to bring it into expression. When you do make the choice to allow it to come into expression, it will flow into your life without much effort. And, as it flows into you as you make this choice, it will then naturally attract the energies to support that flow. I know this is a subtle nuance but right now I would say the most important thing is to make that trusting choice about whether you are ready to truly bring this into this reality.

QUESTION 14: What about teenagers and young adults? Why do they have all these talents and yet seem so stuck, like they just can't move forward in this energy?

SAINT-GERMAIN: The energy right now, as you know, can be very difficult. It is an energy of transition and so often the young ones in particular are waiting for the energies to settle down a little bit before they jump in. They can feel that things are literally moving from one type of energy, a vibrational energy, into something new, an expansional energy, and these young ones don't want to confuse themselves right now by starting their work and expressing their talents in a vibrational energy. They are actually waiting for the expansional energy to become better grounded. That is what they are here to work with so there's no need to push them. I know they get frustrated at times but help them to understand, even through this book, the process that is going on. This also has to do with accepting all that is. Accept that they know for themselves, at some level, why they are waiting.

QUESTION 15: I tried for such a long time to develop my work and, well, it never worked out. I think I chose a long time ago to do this, so now what prevents it from landing on the earth? Why it is so difficult to answer the question "What are you doing"?

SAINT-GERMAIN: So what are you doing?

QUESTIONER 15: Well, I started out trying to teach musicians how to overcome physical problems with more feeling the body, more awareness of the body, and now I am also trying to teach people who are not musicians. But I never have a nice story to explain what I do. In the teaching, or when I have a class, it's very pleasant and I don't have problems talking. But to just to make it visible and make a living from it, it doesn't work. This even showed up in a logo that I designed three years ago. I asked people to help it technically, to put it in the computer, and either they quit or they were not interested or they told me to find another form because it didn't print well. I thought it was the equipment but recently I wondered if there is something wrong with the energy of it?

SAINT-GERMAIN: Yes, there is. When creators create, it is generally done first in the outer etheric realms, sometimes called the crystalline realms. Creation does not begin in this dimension. You go out at night, you draw on things like past life talents, experiences from this life, and you go off into what we're going to call the crystalline kitchen and start putting the ingredients together, mixing them up as the brilliant creator you are. This is when the passion and the desire starts to grow back here in the human reality because you know that you're putting together this wonderful creation. Then you start bringing it to earth, bringing in the ideas, bringing in the essence, the concept. You have the love and creator energy already put into this.

But a funny thing happens when creators bring it into this reality: They tend to control it. They tend to have very defined expectations of success, very defined ideas about how it should work, who should be involved in it, how big it should be, how often it should occur. It brings up all of these human control issues.

You are a wonderful creator – but you're an even better controller. This is one aspect of yourself that you came here to learn about, to learn how to let go of all of those controls. What happens when you control something? It restricts the flow. It cuts down on the potential for the very expression of your creation. The sad part of it is, because you have controlled so much of this, you have very defined ideas of exactly what you think it should be like and therefore you have limited much of the bigger picture, your bigger creation, from flowing into this reality. You have controlled and tightened the pipeline so much that not all of the information can come into this reality. You are suffocating your own creation, you see. And it is a brilliant creation, I wish it had been mine. But there are some aspects to it that haven't even been able to come to earth yet.

Let go of the whole idea now. Let go of it – and we're not saying a little bit or a medium bit. Let go of all of it, completely. It is still yours, you still birthed it, but now let it come to you in a new and different way where it will make sense to you in a different way. Perhaps it will be even packaged and presented to others in a different way.

Take pride and joy in your creation but don't control so much.

QUESTIONER 15: Will I be able to make a living from it, once I come out of this situation?

SAINT-GERMAIN: I'm going to ask you even to take that control off of it. I know the human part of you really wants to know but again it would limit you to put this financial band or requirement around it.

Let me put it this way: You're going to be able to make a living. Now, do you want to do this as well? Do the two have to be together? Do you want them to be together? Don't limit it, don't try to be the Master based on your human needs. The human needs are taken care of, there are many who have already experienced this. Once they let go of focusing on the human needs and instead worked on their creator expression, the human needs just fell into place. Who knows where the money is going to come from? It's just there. When you are in your passion, as you easily can be with this work, the rest is taken care of.

Start all over. Go back to the crystalline realms, to your crystalline kitchen. Stir the pots a little bit more, turn up the heat, smell the essence of your creation, come back to earth, make the choice to bring it in – and then allow it to come in in it's own way, in your higher way.

QUESTION 16: I knew what my life's passion was when I was still a small child but I seem to have chosen a life which has put lots of obstacles in the way and prevented myself from following that. I'm now in a situation where I have acute ear and head pains which are probably connected with my inability to leap into my passion. Could you perhaps say something to this? – because I've had enough.

SAINT-GERMAIN: Indeed. Excellent question, by the way, because it applies to all of Shaumbra. Each of you came into this lifetime with soul passions and desires at many different levels. Remember, as I said, everything has its facets, even passions, soul passions. You can look at your soul passion from many different angles and find many different elements in this passion. When you were young you felt or experienced one particular facet or angle of your soul passion, and it made an impression on you, in every part of you, so you have pursued that and held it as a dream. But there are other aspects of that same soul passion that you haven't necessarily explored yet and now would be a wonderful time to do so.

How do you do that? You simply go into your feelings. What would you like to do? What gives you great pleasure? What fulfills you? Now please, for anyone who is exploring soul passions, do not include other people or communities or countries or the world or the planet or any of these in your consideration. That can often be a false motivator in a passion. If you say "I want to do this work because it will save the world," sorry – you're lacking compassion and you're back in the old martyrdom energy. The greatest service you can be to the world is to be yourself.

I repeat: *The greatest service you can be to the world is to be yourself.*

So when considering your soul passion now, understand that the passion has changed from when you were young. It has changed tremendously because of the era that you are now in, this New Energy era. It is contained within the same jewel of the original passion but it is a different facet that you are looking through now.

The headaches and other physical pains are very temporary, by the way. It is simply the part of your body that is manifesting this feeling of being stuck. Like I said earlier, any time you have physical pain, go in and explore it, accept it, feel it. It is there for a reason and it is trying to tell you something – perhaps that it is time to get unstuck. You will find that it will go away and it will stay away as long as you take a look at your new soul passion, your new desire.

QUESTION 17: I'd like to ask something about my marriage. It's a very difficult marriage, my husband doesn't even know that I'm here doing this. For years I felt safe in my marriage and with my family and my children, but for almost two years I have felt that there is something else in me – but I don't know what it is. I don't know how to do it, how to find what's in me. I am looking for who I am, looking for myself.

SAINT-GERMAIN: Indeed, and you're to be admired for that, not many humans do. Continue.

QUESTIONER 17: Yes, I'm used to doing old things because they are familiar to me but now I feel I have to do some new things, have new experiences, but I don't know how to do it. I don't know what way I should go.

SAINT-GERMAIN: The problem is not with the relationship or with your family, that is just a way of showing you your own aggravation. I'm going to recommend here that you find a way to have your own place to live for a minimum of three months, best for six months. You can explain to your family how much you care for them and love them but you have this need to have your own space right now.

Now don't give reasons why it cannot be done economically or anything else, because you are just putting excuses in the way. There is a desperate cry from yourself that you need your own space, your safe space, in which to blossom. There is a pressure within you right now in your etheric energy that will be in your physical energy soon. It is a pressure that you need to blossom, you need to open up, but you don't feel that you can do it where you are right now. And actually, to move in with friends or relatives wouldn't do it either. You, in particular, need your own space.

Once you have this you're going to know exactly what to do, how to spend the time with yourself – much deserved time with yourself, by the way – and you're going to have a different perspective on your relationship with your family and with yourself. But I want to be very clear that this is something you need to do for yourself so there won't be a physical repercussion or energy backing up in your physical body to cause some sort of imbalance that would be harder to deal with later. It is important that you have your own space. Insist on it.

QUESTIONER 17: At night I'm very afraid to be alone and do things alone because I'm used my husband being with me and having someone there I feel safe with. But...

SAINT-GERMAIN: Safe and suffocated.

QUESTIONER 17: Yeah. But there's also indeed a feeling that I want my own place where I can stay with myself.

SAINT-GERMAIN: Yes. With your own place you're going to find that, for a short period of time it's going to put some of the fears in front of you but they're not that big. You're going to find great delight, actually, in having this time by yourself and doing things like listening to the music that you want to, or sitting in complete quiet, or reading, or any of these gifts that you have not given yourself. You have been serving others, now it is time to let the energy come in and serve you.

And we're going to say very specifically here: *Don't compromise.* Don't go just part way. This is very important. Remember this is not about your family, this is about you. You are perceiving some difficulties with your family but the difficulties are really coming from you who is crying out to have attention.

QUESTIONER 17: My daughter is having a little baby within one and a half months and for the first time I'm a grandma, so that's also in my mind. I know I have to take my own time but I am very curious about the new life, the new child.

SAINT-GERMAIN: Oh, continue to communicate and to be part of your family but always go back to your own space at the end of the day. Wake up in your own space first thing in the morning. Of course have the grandchild come over to play and do all of these other things you're used to doing but there is a need to have your own space. As I said, you're like a flower ready to blossom but you cannot blossom like you need to in your current situation.

Above all, as we began this gathering, we will also end it with the trust in self. The simple, compassionate and total trust in yourself. This is the way of the Master of the New Energy.

I am a Master, and you are also.

OTHER COURSES
by Adamus Saint-Germain

DreamWalker™ Death Transitions
This three-day school, offered by certified teachers, teaches how to guide friends, family and clients through the death process into the nonphysical realms, providing comfort and love to make their transition more peaceful. This School offers certification as a DreamWalker Death Guide.

DreamWalker™ Birth Transitions
This three-day school is offered by certified teachers as well as through a Personal Study Course. Saint-Germain defines the birth process from conception to post-birth with a focus on the spiritual selection aspects. This School offers certification as a DreamWalker "Adoula" Guide.

DreamWalker™ Ascension Transitions
Adamus Saint-Germain's three day Ascension School provides unique and personal insights into the nature of Ascension and the implications of the last lifetime on Earth. This course is offered by certified DreamWalker Ascension teachers.

DreamWalker™ Life
Adamus Saint-Germain's three day DreamWalker Life School provides insights on how to truly live in and love life. Through Quantum Allowing and the grace of the crystal flame of transfiguration, attendees learn what it means to be a Master on Earth. This course is offered by certified DreamWalker DreamWalker Life teachers.

New Energy Synchrotize™
Adamus Saint-Germain says Synchrotize goes "beyond hypnosis" for those who want to consciously create their reality. Synchrotize is offered as a Personal Study Course. The study process takes four consecutive days to complete.

Standard Technology

Adamus Saint-Germain and Tobias join together to present Standard Technology, a New Energy program for activating your body's natural rejuvenation system. Standard Technology is offered as a Personal Study Course.

OTHER COURSES
available through the Crimson Circle

Tobias' Sexual Energies School
This three-day school focuses on what Tobias calls the "sexual energy virus." It helps the student understand how people energetically feed off of others, and how to release the chain of the virus. This is one of the most basic and important courses offered by the Crimson Circle. It is taught by certified teachers worldwide.

Tobias' Journey of the Angels School
Given three weeks before his departure, in this profound school Tobias weaves together the core of all his teachings over the previous 10 years. Offering a completely different perspective on everything you learned in church and school, this school will change your concept of what being human really is.

Single and Multi Session Audio Products Tobias, Kuthumi and Adamus cover a broad range of topics in dozens of recorded presentation. Varying in length from an hour or less to 15 or more hours of channeling, these life-changing sessions are also available with translations in nearly 20 languages.

Monthly Shouds Text transcripts or audio recordings of all monthly Tobias Shouds since August 1999 are available free of charge on the Crimson Circle web site (www.crimsoncircle.com). The Shouds are channeled in annual series (The Creator Series, The New Earth Series, The Divine Human Series, etc.) and also include the live Question and Answer sessions. The Shouds are an excellent record of Shaumbra's journey since the beginning of the Crimson Circle.

Workshops Geoffrey and Linda Hoppe present workshops around the world featuring live Tobias, Saint-Germain and Kuthumi channelings. Check the Crimson Circle web site for dates and details. www.crimsoncircle.com

"I Am, Yes I Am!"

- Adamus Saint-Germain

Printed in Great Britain
by Amazon